# WHAT ARE THE TARGUMS?

# OLD TESTAMENT STUDIES

*Volume 7*

# What Are the Targums?

*Selected texts*

Translated and presented
by
Pierre Grelot

Translated from the French
by
Salvator Attanasio

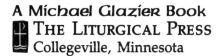
A Michael Glazier Book
THE LITURGICAL PRESS
Collegeville, Minnesota

A Michael Glazier Book published by The Liturgical Press.

Cover design by David Manahan, O.S.B.

This book was originally published in French by Éditions du Cerf under the title *Les Targoums: Textes Choisis,* volume 54 of the series *Les Cahiers Evangile,* copyright © Éditions du Cerf, Paris.

| 1 | 2 | 3 | 4 | 5 | 6 | 7 | 8 | 9 |
| --- | --- | --- | --- | --- | --- | --- | --- | --- |

**Library of Congress Cataloging-in-Publication Data**

Bible. O.T. English. Attanasio. Selections. 1992.
    What are the Targums? : (selected texts) / translated and presented by Pierre Grelot ; translated from the French by Salvator Attanasio.
       p.   cm. — (Old Testament studies ; v. 7)
    Translation of: Les Targoums: Textes Choisis.
    "A Michael Glazier book."
    Includes bibliographical references.
    ISBN 0-8146-5644-7
    1. Bible. O.T. Aramaic—Versions. I. Grelot, Pierre, 1917-
II. Title. III. Series: Old Testament studies (Wilmington, Del.) ; v. 7.
BS709.4.B53   1992
221.4'2—dc20
                                         92-6236
                                           CIP

# CONTENTS

## III. TARGUM OF THE PSALMS AND OF THE FIVE SCROLLS

# FOREWORD

Since the Renaissance biblicists have tried to go beyond the customary translations in order to draw nearer to the original languages: the Hebrew of the Old Testament and the Greek of the New Testament. More recently, however, interest has shifted to the great ancient Jewish translations of the Scriptures: the Septuagint in Greek and the Aramaic Targums. Instead of viewing them as fanciful, bad translations laden with pious popular legends, modern research has learned to read these texts for what they actually are, namely commented translations, testimonies of the Jewish faith. Is not, for that matter, any translation an interpretation? The divergencies between the Hebrew text and its Greek or Aramaic translations are, above all, precious testimonies of the Jewish reading of the Scriptures. Although the Targums cannot exactly be dated, their commitment to writing, from the second century of our era on, must have established a long oral tradition, and a very conservative one inasmuch as it was linked to the transmission of the Scriptures. The Jews who were the contemporaries of Jesus well understood the psalmody of the Hebrew texts in the synagogues of Galilee, but they understood and memorized only the Targums and their commentaries developed in the homilies.

Pierre Grelot has taught Aramaic for a long time at the Catholic Institute of Paris. A specialist in the study of Targums, he has translated and edited several of them. Of these texts he has selected sixty, many of which are little known or scattered in rare and scholarly works. His presentation facilitates a reading of these texts and points out their interest for the study of both the Old and the New Testament. Thus he permits the modern reader to approach the Bible used by Jesus and the first Christians by giving ear to the resonances of the Word of God in the living tradition of the Jewish people.

                                                    Phillipe Gruson

# THE TARGUMS

The word Targum passed into Aramaic and then into Hebrew from the Akkadian: *Targumanu* was the "interpreter": he himself was designated by a word of foreign (Hittite) origin. It is employed in Judaism by an entire genre of the rabbinic literature that offers "interpretative translations." The sacred books lie steadfastly at the base of the interests of this genre. It is a matter of making them intelligible to people who do not understand either written or spoken Hebrew. It is *interpretative* because it is not a question, not always anyway, of literal translations, but the reading of texts in which an interpretation of the original is incorporated by means of major or minor amplifications. It is not, properly speaking, a *midrash,* that is to say an "explanation" added to biblical verses cited in their literalness. Rather, it is often the offspring of such verses, creatively interpreted and freely utilized for the instruction and the edification of listeners and readers. In the legislative books the amplifications of the texts can take the form of a *Halaka,* a juridical explanation that "binds." Everywhere they derive from a much freer *haggada* which pads, as it were, the original by adding materials borrowed from oral tradition in unforeseeable proportions. All the biblical books possess Targums, except those that already include Aramaic passages, namely, Daniel, Ezra and Nehemiah. Some possess several such passages (the Pentateuch and Esther). The targumic achievement is a copious one. But its function must be located carefully in order to understand its prolificy and its internal variety.

## The Targum and the Liturgical Reading of Scripture

The Targum is closely linked to the liturgical reading of Scripture, but it is not certain that such is generally the case. For example, Cave XI at Qumran has yielded the remains of a rather literal Targum of Job: it is not at all sure whether it had been intended that it should accompany the reading of the book in the liturgical assemblies. It seems, rather, that it involves a literary work of a particular genre for private use. On the other hand, the fragments of a Targum of Leviticus (Cave IV) are probably connected with a liturgical lectionary of which only fragments remain. At all events, even at Qumran these fragments attest the felt need to make the biblical text intelligible to people who no longer understand classical Hebrew. The inroad of Aramaic among the Jewish people is an occurrence posterior to the exile, contemporaneous with the expansion of this language as the official language of the chancellories of the Persian Empire. The most ancient trace of an oral interpretation accompanying the public reading of the Law is found in the book of Nehemiah at the moment of the proclamation of the Law by Ezra: the Levites "explained the Law of God, translating and giving it meaning so that the people understood what was being read" (Neh. 8, 8).

The event took place in the Temple. In addition we must picture to ourselves analagous scenes in gatherings of the synagogue, wherever Hebrew was no longer in common use. We can grasp the progression only retrospectively, from the laws laid down by rabbinic Judaism. Since it concerns a very fundamental fact in terms of tradition, scholars build on this practice that developed later in order to get an idea of the ancient practice.

The Targum is applied to all the texts read officially in the synagogal gathering: the Law (or Torah) first of all, then the *haftaroth,* prophetic fragments selected with respect to the reading of the Law. The rule requires that the reading be made first in the original text from a *written* book so that the sacred text is fully respected. Afterwards, verse by verse, as regards the Torah, with lengthier passages as regards the prophets or other writings from which excerpts could be drawn, the targumist gives an oral interpretation by following the givens of the tradition. Nowhere is it said that it is forbidden to commit these Targums to writing. But the targumist is forbidden to have a written text in front of him when he provides his interpretation so that the latter will not be confused with sacred Scripture. Hence remembrance plays an essential role in the transmission of this interpretative tradition. But we can rely on its fidelity in a cultural framework in which writing has not yet supplanted the oral tradition, as is the case

in the modern West. Thus the Targum is the product of a practical need and it developed in the framework of this practical need,
having as its essential role the transmission of the meaning of
Scripture, and utilizing for this purpose all the lateral elements
that appeared useful. Accordingly a certain freedom was taken
in the recourse to "edifying" development that could pad Scripture itself. The fundamental concern for fidelity leaves full room
for a "living" reading in which the actuality of the texts is made
fully evident.

## The Targums of the Torah

In the present state of affairs there exist three Targums of the
Torah (or Pentateuch). The most ancient one has never been fixed
definitively. Based upon an ancient oral tradition that was taught
in the rabbinic schools of Galilee from the second century on,
it bears the name Targum *Yerushalmi* (= of Jerusalem). Up to
around 1950 it was known only in a fragmentary form, thanks
to the collections of more or less lengthy "fragments" gathered
in particular manuscripts and fragments restored by the *Cairo
Gueniza.* A complete manuscript, however, was found by A. Diez
Macho in the Vatican Library (Ms. *Neofiti I*), which itself contains marginal and interlineal glosses. Hence from now on it will
be possible to apply onself to a precise work of analysis of its
text, represented by four different recensions. At times its ortho-
graphy has been modernized, but its text has been substantially
well preserved.

A second Targum of the Torah tended to draw its text closer
to the original Hebrew, and the Jewish academies of Babylon con-
ferred upon it an official value around the third century: this is
the so-called Targum of Onkelos. It contains still some *amplifications* in certain Haggadic passages but its *Halaka* aligns itself
strictly with that of the rabbinic tradition. It is conceivably of
Palestinian origin. But it is written in a dialect different from that
of the *Yerushalmi,* a dialect close to the classic "Aramaic" of
Daniel.

Finally, a later composition, to which the name *Yerushalmi I*
(TJ¹) or Pseudo-Jonathan (P.J.) is given, took over whole fragments of the Tg. *Yerushalmi,* inserting them in a framework that
followed the Tg. of Onkelos and adding midrashic passages whose

sources are traceable. It contains very ancient fragments, but it also gives the names of Mahomet's daughters, which pushes its composition back to the late Middle Ages. In the passages in which it parallels Codex *Neofiti I* and the fragmentary Tg. (TJ²), it remains a lateral testimony of the Tg. *Yerushalmi*.

## The Targum of the Prophets

In the present state of documentation, the Targum of the Prophets (ancient and recent = Joshua up to 2 Kings, then Isaiah, Jeremiah, Ezra, and the Twelve) was fixed in the same milieu as the Targum of Onkelos with recourse to the same Aramaic dialect, with the intention of conferring upon it officially a similar value for synagogal reading. It is first mentioned in a rabbinic saying of the third century. But, at times the manuscripts contain additional fragments in their margins that bear the title: "Targum *Yerushalmi*" or "other Targum." The fragments in question bear on important passages which from a very early date must have formed part of the synagogal "lectionary." In these developed passages the text of the Torah, to which they were added, is often discernible.

This does not, however, mean to say that before the Tg. was promulgated officially under the name of Jonathan there probably existed a complete Targum *Yerushalmi* of the Prophets. But a Targum of the Lessons (*haftaroth*), selected to accompany the different fragments of the Torah, must have existed very early. It is in these passages, the great antiquity of which is not necessarily guaranteed, that the most Haggadic developments are found. The Tg. of Jonathan tends to follow the Hebrew text while taking various liberties with it. At times one suspects the existence of a Tg. *Yerushalmi* behind it. And, indeed, some traces of it are present. For example, behind the targum of Is. 63, 1, one can divine the existence of a more ancient text that interpreted this text in a messianic way as in Rev. 19, 13. In fact, this interpretation is presumed by the Tg. *Yerushalmi* of Gen. 49, 13-14. In a general way, it is the Tg. of Isaiah which is the richest in developments. Elsewhere they are more dispersed (except for the prayer of Habakkuk (Hab. 3). A tinge of anti-Christian apologetic appears in it (for example, in Is. 52, 13-53, 12). On the whole the

Tg. of the Prophets is a good witness to rabbinical theology, which has pre-Christian substructures in a good number of cases.

## The Targum of "Megillot" (or Five Scrolls)

The Five Scrolls (the Song of Songs, Ruth, Lamentations, Ecclesiastes, and Esther) occupy a place apart in the Targums. The primitive text is particularly amplified in them, so that the Targum turns often to the Aramaic Midrash. Occasionally the echo of ancient traditions can be found in it, but in its present form the text is relatively recent. The language that predominates in it is the Aramaic called "of Galilee," the same as in the Tg. *Yerushalmi* of the Pentateuch. But there is more than a trace of the Tg. of Onkelos present, perhaps in consequence of the activity of the copyists. Esther is a case apart. It is known that it was the only biblical book that each family had a right to own; it was read at home on the occasion of the Purim festival. Thus it is understandable that targumic activity particularly attached itself to the book of Esther in a written form. In fact there are three Targums to this single book. One (the Tg. III) is very literal: it is to be found only in the Antwerp *Polyglot* and its foundational manuscript has disappeared. Another (the Tg. II) is a very developed Haggadic midrash written in the Aramaic "of Galilee." It even contains several poems in "alphabetical" form which betray its carefully crafted literary composition. The third (Tg. I) is an amplification that glosses the Tg. III, respecting its foundational text but considerably amplifying the Hebrew of the book. It is probably the most recent of the three, although it is impossible to fix dates. Moreover there are in the manuscripts different transpositions between Tgs. I and II. Save for the Tg. III of Esther, we are at the antipodes of simple translation: the Tgs. of the Megillot are works of an edifying literature.

## The Targums of the "Writings"

There are also Targums of the Psalms, Job, Proverbs, and Chronicles. The latter exists only in three manuscripts. But recently it was the subject of a critical edition prepared by R. Le Déaut (thanks to a manuscript in the Vatican Library until then neglected).

As regards Job and the Psalms, the text has never been strictly fixed. In a number of places the manuscripts give two or three paraphrases for the same verse. This does not mean that two or three complete Tgs. existed, from which these variants might have been taken, but that traditional explanation given of the texts was used to a plurality of interpretation and was respected by the collectors. The manuscripts, moreover, are divided into several families. Thus the Antwerp and London *Polyglots* do not coincide at every point: the London *Polyglot,* for example, reproduces the rabbinic Venice Bible.

The Psalms, represented by a great number of manuscripts, really require a detailed study. It is for this reason no doubt that they are absent from the critical edition of the Targums published by A. Sperber. We find in them, more than once, haggadic amplifications that presume a whole commentary. Is the commentary ancient? We cannot be sure because the Tg. is written in a "mixed" dialect. The targumists tend to generalize the Davidic origin of the Psalms, for example in regard to Ps. 110 from which messianism is excluded. But there are exceptions; for example, Ps. 45, which is interpreted as messianic. Some Psalms are very amplified, for example, Ps. 18 and Ps. 68.

Outside the books of the Hebrew Bible, the Targum of several deuterocanonical books, translated from the Greek, should likewise be mentioned: such is the case with Tobit, with Mordecai's dream and Esther's prayer (book of Esther), and supplements of Daniel (taken from Theodotion's translation). The texts are late.

## For a Considered Choice of Targumic Texts

The ensemble of the Targums is much lengthier than the totality of the Old Testament. Thus a considered choice must be made in order to present a proper idea of them. What is essential is to be aware of the work done by the targumist on the texts which they had to interpret. Accordingly cases of simple translations can be set aside. The most interesting cases for the Christian reader are those in which the haggada is liberally developed, either because its content or lateral attestations allow one to regard them as pre-Christian, or because in them are some features discernible that betray a reaction to the Christian use of the Scriptures. The choice of Torah texts is usually a better choice than that of the Prophets. The Psalms and the Five Scrolls will provide their contingent of texts. Each fragment will be accompanied by indispensable notes, but not by a commentary, which would require lengthy explanations. The translations will be as literal as possible. In some cases the translation of the Hebrew text will be given first, so that one can better appreciate the labor exerted by the targumists in order to interpret it—or to give it a meaning, possibly different from the one it had in the beginning. The words of the passages that correspond to the Hebrew text are in italics.

# I

# THE TARGUMS
# OF THE LAW

# 1

# THE SENTENCES OF GOD
## Tg. of Genesis 3, 14-19

For the narrative of the original sin, the Targum follows the Hebrew text rather closely. It amplifies it at the end, in particular as regards the sentence pronounced upon the serpent. On the whole the text is that of the manuscript *Neofiti I* (N) except for the final addition.

> [14]*YHWH—God said to the Serpent: "Because you have done that, you shall be accursed, Serpent, among the cattle and among all wild beasts. You shall crawl on your belly and dust shall be your nourishment every day of your life.* [15]*And I will put enmity between you and your wife,* between her descendants and your descendants. And it shall come to pass that when her descendants shall keep the Law and observe my commandments, they shall rise against you, *they shall smite your head* and they shall kill you. And when they shall forsake the commandments of the Law, you shall rise against them, *you will bite his[a] (?) heel* and you shall wound him (?). But for his descendants there shall be a healing and for you, Serpent, there will be no healing. [But they must make peace with each other come the days of the King Messiah] (TJ²)."[b]

The sentence pronounced upon the woman follows the Hebrew text, except for the addition at the end:

> [16]". . . and he will have power over you, be it to justify, be it to sin."

[a]Here the plural would be expected.

[b]Here there is a perspective of hope, a kind of "protogospel."

The sentence upon Adam[c] adds at the end:

> [18]". . . *and you shall eat the grass that is in the field.*" Adam
> replied and said: "I pray that, through your very own mercy,
> YHWH, we not be considered as cattle so as to eat the grass
> of the field! Let us rise up then and let us toil and by the toil
> of our hands we shall eat as nourishment the fruits of the
> ground. In that way, there will be a difference between cattle
> and men." [19]"*By the sweat of your face you shall eat bread*
> *until you return to the ground, for from it were you created.*
> *For you are dust and to dust you must return.* But you must
> return from the dust and rise up again,[d] and then render an
> explanation of all that which you will have done."

Here in place of the "garments of the skin" (Hebrew text) God,
with the serpent's skin, fashioned for Adam and his wife "garments of glory." This garment fashioned for Adam was to have
a history: it was to pass on to Enoch, to Noah, to Sem, to Abraham, who finally was to give it to Joseph. Obviously this singu-
larly enriches the primitive text. The continuation is no less amplified.

[c]The Tg. says Adam where the Hebrew says "man."
[d]Perspective of final resurrection with a view to the Last Judgment.

# 2

# THE MYTH OF THE TREE OF LIFE
## Tg. of Genesis 3, 22-24

In Genesis the Tree of Life is an element derived from ancient
oriental myths. The Targum develops these elements so as to link
praise of the Law to it. The text is drawn from the Codex *Neofiti*
*I,* but on several occasions its marginal glosses (gl) which coincide with the fragmentary Targum (TJ[2]) are followed.

[22]And [the Word of God said] (gl and TJ[2]): Behold the first Adam whom I created is alone in the world as I am alone in the heaven above. Numerous nations are going to arise from him and from him shall arise a people that *will know* how to distinguish between *Good* and *Evil*. If he had kept the prescriptions of the Law and observed its commandments, he would have lived and subsisted like the Tree of Life for centuries. Now, since he has not kept the prescriptions of the Law nor observed its commandments (it is proper that we expel him from the Garden of Eden before he *stretches forth his hand and seizes* the fruits *of the Tree of Life, and before he eats of it and lives for ever.* [23]And the Word of God (gl and TJ[2]) *expelled him from the Garden of Eden in order to cultivate the ground from which he had been created.* [24]*And he expelled Adam and he made* the glory of his Presence dwell, from the beginning, *east of the Garden of Eden* between the two *cherubs.*

Two thousand years before he had created the world, he had created the Law[a] and he had established the Garden of Eden for the just so that they may eat and rejoice in the fruit of the Tree, because they will have kept the prescriptions of the Law in this world below and observed his commandments. He arranged Gehenna for the wicked for it is comparable to a sharp sword devouring from both sides. In the middle of it he set bolts of fire and live coals for the wicked so that revenge be taken upon them in the world to come because they did not keep the prescriptions of the Law in this world below. For the Law is a *Tree of Life*[b] for whoever strives toward it and observes its commandments: he lives and subsists like the Tree of life in the world to come. The Law is good for those who practice it in this world below as are the fruits of the Tree of Life.

The Hebrew text has a much more accentuated "mythic" aspect than its targumic paraphrase, namely, in v. 24 where only fragments are to be found. The targumist introduces the theme of the Law, the source of life, along with that of the two-fold retribution of the just and the wicked (or impious), both totally absent from the primitive text. But these are two themes equally important in rabbinic theology, where both the primitive crea-

[a]That forms part of the ten things created before the world.
[b]Cf. Pr. 3, 13 (on the subject of Wisdom).

tion of the Law and the theme of the Garden of Eden are found. Since the theme of the two-fold retribution is found in the Gospel, one can be assured of its antiquity.

# 3

# CAIN AND ABEL
## Tg. of Genesis 4, 3-16

The targumic development of this story is unequal from verse to verse. Here those verses that are most amplified are cited. The total text is taken from a manuscript of the *Cairo Gueniza* published by P. Kahle, except for the beginning and the end which are missing. Thus recourse to the manuscript *Neofiti I* (N) is necessary, which also furnishes some supplementary details.

[3]It came to pass at the end of a certain time that Cain brought fruits of the ground as offering in the name of YHWH (N). [4]And Abel also brought the firstlings of his little flock and of the fat thereof. Now, the Word of the Lord accepted with favor Abel and his offering, [5]but it did not accept with favor Cain and his offering. Cain was very displeased and aspect his face changed. [6]The Word of the Lord said to Cain: "Why then are you so displeased and why then has the aspect of your face changed? [7]Is it not true that if you rectify your works [in this world below] (N) it will be remitted to you and forgiven to you in the world to come, *and if you do not rectify your works* in this world, your sin is retained for the great Judgment?[a] *But sin is crouched at the door* of the heart, and I have remitted in your hands the control of the wicked inclination,[b] and you yourself *have power over it,* be it to sin, be it to act rightly.

[8]Now Cain said to Abel his brother: "Come and let us both go out into the open field. *And it came to pass,* when *they* both

---

[a]Compare Jn. 20, 23, (same expression).

[b]The good and the evil inclinations are themes of rabbinic theology.

*had come to the open field,* that Cain began to speak and said to Abel: "I see that the world has not been created by love, and that it is not ruled by love [and that there is partiality toward persons at the Judgment] (N). Why then was your offering accepted with favor and mine not accepted with favor?" Abel replied and said to Cain: "I declare [I] (N) that the world was created by love and that it is ruled by love. But it is ruled according to the fruit of good works. Because my works were better than yours, my offering was accepted with favor and as for yours, it was not accepted with favor." [Cain replied and said to Abel: "There is no Judgment, no Judge, no other world. There is no gift of reward to the just nor of punishment for the wicked." Abel replied and said to Cain: "There is a Judgment, and there is a Judge, and there is another world, and there is the gift of a reward to the just and a punishment for the wicked in the world to come]. (N) And the two of them quarreled in the open field. *And Cain rose against Abel his brother and slew him.*

Verses 9 to 14 follow the Hebrew text with slight additions: it is the dialogue between Cain and God. Cain is desperate over his crime. Nevertheless, he confesses that God has the power to remit and to forgive. Finally God swears to him that Judgment shall be suspended over the head of the one who makes an attempt on Cain's life, unto seven generations.

To conclude:

> [16]*Cain went out from the presence of the Lord* and he dwelt on the ground, exiled and vagabond, to the *east* of the garden of *Eden.* And it came to pass, before he slew his brother Abel, that the ground produced fruits like those of the garden of Eden. But after he had slain Abel [it changed and produced in his presence thorns and brambles]. (N)

The story of the enemy brothers is transformed here in order to present two literary types: the just who performs good works, and the impious whose works are wicked. The impious does not believe in the love of God, nor in the Judgment (here below and beyond the grave), nor in future retribution. The just professes the exact faith on all these points. One wonders whether the men thus alluded to are pagan philosophers, whose thought was not unknown to the Jews, or a category of sceptical Jews. In the latter case, it could be a pharisaic polemic against the Sadducees who did not believe in a future life. But in this case they would be the butt of caricature. Two important connections with the New Testament will be noted. One concerns only the religious vocabulary: sins can either be forgiven and remitted, or retained (cf. Jn. 20, 23). The other is more important because it shows that the targumic tradition was known and current: it is the example of Cain cited 1 Jn. 3, 12. Cain, it is said, slit his brother's throat because Cain's works were wicked, whereas those of his brother were just. It is exactly the situation described here in the margins of the Genesis text.

# 4

# THE VISIONS OF ABRAHAM
## Tg. of Genesis 15, 1-17

The praise of the faith of Abraham (Abram before chapter 17) and the narrative of his covenant with God give rise to considerable amplifications. First to be noted are the patriarch's reflections on the doctrine of retribution, then two visions artificially linked to the Genesis narrative. Here we are following the text of Codex *Neofiti I*. Several marginal glosses and the fragmentary Targum (TJ²) would add variants and additions. The Pseudo-Jonathan (TJ¹) approximately follows the same text.

> ¹*After these events,* when were assembled all the kingdoms of the earth that had waged war against Abraham and that had fallen before him, when he had slain four kings among them and had returned with nine encampments[a] Abram thought in his heart and said to himself: "Woe is me! Perhaps I have received the reward of the commandments in this world below and I will have no share of the world to come. Or perhaps the

[a]Reference to the campaign that is related in Ch. 4.

brethren or the next of kin of the victims who fell before me
are going to return to their citadels and their cities, numerous
legions will join them and they will come against me and slay
me. Or perhaps there was in my grasp the fulfillment of some
precepts, at the previous time when they fell before me, and
that played in my favor. Or perhaps the fulfillment of a commandment, the second time, will not be in my grasp, and the
name of the Heavens will be profaned on account of me." This
is why *a* prophetic *word was addressed* from the immediate
vicinity of YHWH to *Abram* the just, *saying:* "*Fear not,
Abram,* even if numerous legions gather and come against you
to slay you, my Word *will be a shield for you,* for it will be
a protection for you in this world. And even if I have delivered
your enemies before you in this world, *the reward* of your good
works is prepared for you before me in the world to come."
*²Abram said:* "I pray you, for the sake of your own love,
YHWH, you have given me much and you have before you
much *to give me.* But I, I go *childless* out of this world, and
Eliezer, the son of my house through whose hand signs were
made for me at Damascus, will be my heir."

Verses 3–6 approximately follow the Hebrew in order to praise
Abram's faith. Thus we arrive at the ceremonial of the covenant:

"... He said to him: 'I am YHWH who has brought you
out of the fiery furnace of the Chaldeans*ᵇ* in order to give you
this land as inheritance.' ⁸He said, 'I pray you, for the sake
of your own love, whereby shall I know that I inherit it?' He
said to him 'Offer before me a heifer of three years old, a she-
goat of three years old, a ram of three years old, a turtle-dove
and a young pigeon.' He offered them before him. He cut them
in two and laid each part side by side. But he did not cut the
birds in two. When some birds came down upon the parts, the
merit of Abraham drove them away. When birds of prey came
down, they perched upon the parts. What are these birds of
prey? They are impure birds of prey. And what are these impure birds of prey? They are the kingdoms of the earth: when
they scheme wicked plans against the house of Israel, though
the merit of Abram their father, [God] saves them. ¹²*The sun*

*ᵇ*A play on words on the Ur of the Chaldeans.

was about to set. A gentle sleep fell upon Abram. And lo, Abram beheld four kingdoms that were rising before him: *a fear*, it is Babylon; *from the darkness*, it is Media; *huge*, it is Greece; *fell upon him*, it is Edom the perverse which must fall without the power to rise.

Verses 13–16 are practically translated literally. But the Targum adds a second vision of Abram in v. 17:

> [17]*And behold the sun set and it was twilight* and this is what Abraham beheld when seats were being arranged and thrones set in place. And lo, Gehenna, which is comparable to a fiery furnace caused to flare flames of fire, sparks *of fire* in the midst of which fell sinners, because they had rebelled against the Law during their life in this world below. But the just, because they had kept the Law, were saved from anguish. All was thus shown to Abram as he *passed among these parts*.

The final end of the chapter is translated literally. The meaning of the three additions becomes clear. The first (v. 1) shows that God's promise responds to an anguish felt by the patriarch: it is that which arouses his faith, recalling moreover (v. 7), that God had saved him previously from the "fiery furnace of the Chaldeans" (this play on words on the name of Ur furnished the subject of an entire narrative). The second addition (vv. 11–12) interprets the text word for word by introducing the theory of the four kingdoms (cf. Dan. 2 and 7): Rome ( = Edom in cryptic language) is the last of all. The third addition (v. 17) presents the Last Judgment in a scenario borrowed from Daniel (cf. Dan.), announcing the fate respectively in store for the just and sinners. The text of Genesis thus becomes a pretext for doctrinal expositions based upon its symbolical interpretation.

# 5

# ABRAHAM'S TEST AND THE BINDING OF ISAAC
## Tg. of Genesis 22, 1-14

The narrative of Gen. 22 is a choice item for the Targum. The rabbinic tradition attributed a particular merit to the "binding" of Isaac, with a view to the salvation of his descendants. Here we shall cite the amplification of v. 1 which is found in Pseudo-Jonathan (Ps-J): it has a parallel in an ancient fragment of *Midrash Rabba* on Genesis. Following that, we shall take the text of *Neofiti I,* skipping the verses that almost literally follow the Hebrew text.

> (Ps-J) ¹*It came to pass after these events,* when Isaac and Ishmael quarreled that Ishmael said: "It is my due to inherit from my father, because I am his first-born son." Isaac said: "It is my due to inherit from my father, because I am the son of Sarah his wife, and you, the son of Hagar, my mother's maidservant." Ishmael replied and said: "I am much more deserving than you, for I was circumcised at the age of thirteen,[a] and if it had been my desire to refuse, I would not have given myself up to be circumcised. But you, you were circumcised when you were eight days old.[b] If you had been aware of this, perhaps you would not have delivered yourself up to be circumcised." Isaac replied and said: "Here I am thirty-seven, and if the Holy One (Blessed be He!) were to demand all my limbs, I would not object thereto." Immediately these words were heard before the Master of the world, and immediately the Word of YHWH *put Abraham to the test and said: "Abraham!" He said: "Here I am."*

Thus the Targum explains the reason for Abraham's test, by dwelling more on Isaac's merit. On the other hand, the Codex *Neofiti I* and the fragmentary Tg. dwell on Abraham's person.

[a]Cf. Gen. 17, 23.
[b]Cf. Gen. 21, 4.

(N) *"It came to pass after these events that YHWH put Abraham to the test through the tenth temptation and he said to him: "Abraham!"* Abraham replied in the language of the sanctuary[c] and Abraham *said to him: "Here I am."*

The narrative continues in an almost literal translation, up to the moment in which the dialogue undergoes amplifications.

[7]. . . . [Isaac] said: *Here is the fire and the wood, but where is the lamb for the holocaust?* Abraham said: "Before YHWH a lamb for the holocaust has been prepared for him. If not, you are the lamb of the holocaust" *and they both set forth together* with a perfect heart. [9]*They came to the place of which YHWH had told him and Abraham built an altar there. He laid out the wood, bound his son Isaac and placed him on the altar upon the wood.* [10]*And Abraham stretched forth his hand and took the knife to sacrifice Isaac his son.* Isaac began to speak and said to Abraham his father: "My father, bind me well lest I upset you and your offering be made invalid and I be hurled in the pit of perdition in the world to come." Abraham's eyes turned toward the eyes of Isaac and Isaac's eyes turned toward the angels above. Isaac saw them and Abraham did not see them: at this very moment an echo came down from the heavens and said: "Come and behold the only two (just) souls that there be in the world. The one sacrifices and the other is sacrificed. The one who sacrifices does not object thereto and the one who is being sacrified offers his neck."

[11]*And the angel of YHWH called to him from the heavens and said: "Abraham!"* [Abraham replied in the language of the sanctuary] (gl): *"Here I am."* [12]*He said; "Stretch forth not your hand upon the lad and do him no harm, for I know now that you fear YHWH and that you have not refused your son, your one and only."*

[13]*Abraham raised his eyes and he saw and behold there was a ram* among the trees, *caught by his horns. Abraham went forth to fetch it and to offer it as holocaust in place of his son.* [14] *And Abraham* worshipped and prayed *in the name of the word of* YHWH, and he said: "I pray you for the sake of your own love YHWH. Everything is uncovered and known before you.

[c]Reply in Hebrew.

Now, there was no division in my heart at the moment when you told me to sacrifice Isaac my son and to turn him into dust and ashes before you. But I immediately arose at dawn and fulfilled your Word with joy and executed your decision. But now [I pray you through your own mercy] (TJ2) when the descendants of Isaac find themselves in a time of distress, remember the binding of Isaac their father and hear the voice of their supplication. Hearken to them and deliver them from all tribulation. For the generations to come shall say: "*On the mountain* of the sanctuary of YHWH where Abraham offered Isaac his son, on that mountain to him *appeared* the glory of the Presence of YHWH."

The mention of the language of the sanctuary in Abraham's replies belong rightfully to the Codex *Neofiti I*. The mention of the tenth test (or temptation) of Abraham presumes a list that is found in the *Midrash Rabba* on Genesis. The theme of Isaac, the lamb of the holocaust, may prefigure that of Christ, the Lamb of God (1 Pet. 1, 19 f. Jn. 1, 36). The dwelling upon Isaac's voluntary submission explains the fact that Jewish prayer appeals to his "binding" in order to obtain God's favor. In v. 10 the mention of Isaac's vision explains why he has become blind (see Tg. of Lev. 22, 26-27, p. 50). In v. 13 Mt. Moriah is identified instead of the Temple of Jerusalem.

# 6

# THE THREE LESSONS OF GOD
## Tg. of Genesis 35, 8-10

It is on the occasion of the death of Deborah, Rebekah's nurse, that the targumist presents three acts of God as examples for human beings.

> ⁸*At that time Deborah, Rebekah's nurse died. She was buried under the oak tree, and the oak tree was named: the Ouk*

*of Tears.* ⁹Eternal God, blessed be your name for ever and ever! Since the beginning you have let your gentleness be known to the generations of the world. For your gentleness, your rectitude, your justice, your honor, your praise, your strength and your glory shall never cease. You have taught us excellent commandments and admirable laws.

You have taught us to bless the husband and the wife, since Adam and his companion. For it is thus that the Book explains and says: "And God blessed them and God said to them: 'Increase and multiply, and replenish the earth and subdue it.' "*ᵃ* And the Word of YHWH blessed them, and the Word of YHWH said to them: "Become powerful and multiply, and replenish the earth and subdue it."

And you have further taught us why we are to visit the sick, since our father Abraham, the just, when you appeared to him in your merciful goodness. You had ordered him to circumcise his foreskin, and he had seated himself in front of his tent, in the heat of the day, and you, master of all time YHWH, in your merciful goodness, you appeared to him in order to heal him. For it is thus that the Book explains and says: "And YHWH appeared to him."*ᵇ* And the Word of YHWH appeared to him on the Plain of the Vision, and he, he was seated at the entrance to his tent in the heat of the day.

And you taught us also to console people in mourning. Since our father Jacob, when you appeared to him upon his arrival from Paddan-Aram, the common fate of the world overtook Deborah, the nurse of Rebekah his mother. At this very moment, he was notified that Rebekah his mother was dead. And since the pain in his thigh had not yet been relieved,*ᶜ* Rachel died close to him on the way.*ᵈ* He sat down then, weeping, wailing, grieving and shedding tears. And you, Master of all time, Lord, in your merciful goodness you appeared to him to console him and you pronounced the funerary blessing upon Rebekah his mother according to which it is said: "And the Word of YHWH appeared *to Jacob* a second time upon his

---

*ᵃ*Quotation from Gen. 1, 28 in Hebrew.

*ᵇ*Quotation from Gen. 18, 1 in Hebrew.

*ᶜ*Cf. Gen. 32, 32 (Jacob's struggle with the angel).

*ᵈ*Gen. 35, 19.

*arrival from Paddam-Aram and he blessed him.*[e] [10]And the
Word of YHWH said to him: *"Your name is Jacob. But your
name shall no longer be called Jacob: Israel shall be your
name." And he called him with the name of Israel.*[f]

The text cited here is taken from a papyrus of the *Cairo Gueniza*
(Fragment C of the collection published by P. Kahle). The other
witnesses present slight variations. A marginal gloss of the *Neofiti I* adds a last example:

> (G1) . . . You have also taught us to bury the dead, since our
> master Moses whom the Master of all time YHWH has buried.
> Blessed be his name for ever and ever.

This addition refers to Dt. 34, 6 in the Tg. of the Pseudo-
Jonathan. It completes the collection of examples given by God
to human beings. But it is not in its place at the end of v. 9 where
the Targum reconnects with the biblical text after a development
that incorporates this text. Parallels to this text have been pointed
out in the Talmud. But it is not to be excluded that here the Talmud depends upon the targumic tradition, attached to the beginning of a liturgical pericope.

[e]Quotation of Gen. 35, 9 in Hebrew.
[f]Quotation of Gen. 35, 10, in Hebrew.

# 7

# THE JUST TAMAR
## Tg. of Genesis 38, 24-26

The story of Tamar is well-known. Desperate at the realization
that she has no child and that the levirate law does not apply to
her, she disguises herself as a prostitute and engages in carnal inter-
course with Judah, her father-in-law, who promised her a young
goat. As a pledge she lets him give her his seal, his cloak, and
his stick. Then she disappears and puts on her widow's clothing

again. The text translated here comes from a manuscript of the *Cairo Gueniza* (Fragment D, in the collection of P. Kahle), except for the end taken from the Codex *Neofiti I* (N).

> [24]*It came to pass at the end of three months that an informer told Jedah, saying; "Your daughter-in-law has prostituted herself and lo she has conceived children from prostitution."* Judah said: *"Take her outdoors and burn her."* [25]This Tamar therefore went out to be burned by fire. She looked for the three object-witnesses and did not find them. Thereupon she raised her eyes toward the heights and said: "It is you, YHWH, who hearkens to the prayer of people in distress in their distress. You then, hearken to my prayer in this hour. And I, I am going to arouse for you three just persons on the plain of Doura: Hananyah, Mishael, and Azaryah."[a] At the same moment, YHWH beckoned to Michael and said to him: "Go down and give them back to her." Her eyes were then cleared: she saw them, took them and threw them at the feet of the judges and she said: "*The man to whom they belong is the one by whom I am pregnant.* But even on the edge of the stake, I do not wish to denounce him. I put my trust in the Master of all time, YHWH, for he will place in the heart of the man to whom these things belong recognition of this seal, this cloak and this stick."
> When Judah saw these three object-witnesses, he rose to his feet, cried out and said: "Listen to me, my brethren and men of the house of my father! By the measure with which a man measures, it will be measured to him, be it to a good measure, be it to a bad measure, and blessed be any man whose works are made manifest. It is better for me that I should blush in this world rather than in the world to come. It is better for me that I burn in an extinguishable fire, and not in a fire that devours fire. It is because I took the cloak of my brother Joseph, which I soaked in the blood of a he-goat and sent it to my father, and that I said to him: "*Recognize now,* if it be the cloak of your son Joseph or not. Measure for measure and judgment for judgment! My daughter Tamar is more just than I. (Continuation in N:)/ "It is by me that she is pregnant. Far is Tamar my daughter-in-law from having conceived children of prostitution!" An echo came down from heaven and said: "Both are

[a]Cf. Dan. 3.

justified, the matter is coming before YHWH." *²⁶Judah recognized them and said:* "Tamar my daughter-in-law is innocent. *It is because I did not marry her to Shelak my son.*" And he *knew her no longer again.*

Judah was caught in his own trap. Measure for measure! We recognize here the maxim that is likewise cited in Mt. 7, 2. Did Matthew borrow it from the Targum, or does it refer to a popular saying cited in the two cases? As regards the essence of the question, the Targum makes the meaning of the biblical text explicit. Tamar was within her right, and Judah providentially exercised his levirate authority as the closest relative, by giving rise to a progeny for his deceased son. The heavenly voice proclaims that both are justified. The matter is not without significance for the presence of Tamar in the genealogy of Jesus according to Matthew (Mt. 1, 3). We may wonder whether the targumic tradition is not anterior to the New Testament.

# 8

# THE PROFESSION OF FAITH OF THE TRIBES
## Tg. of Genesis 49, 1-2

Chapter 49 of Genesis, which presents Jacob's blessings, offers a subject amenable to lengthy development. It begins with a context which develops the two first verses: "Gather together, that I may declare to you what lies before you in the days to come. Gather together, listen, sons of Jacob, listen to Israel your father" (49, 1-2). The Targum still has some relation to the beginning of the text, but the end is totally changed.

> *¹Jacob summoned his son and said to them:* "Gather together *and I will declare to you* the hidden mysteries, the secret dates, the retribution allotted to the just, the punishment of the impious and that which shall be the happiness of Eden." The twelve

tribes gathered together and surrounded the golden bed in which our father Jacob laid since the appointed time had been revealed to him so that the appointed time of the blessing and of the consolation be announced to them. After the appointed time had been made known to him, the secret had been hidden from him. They thought that he was going to declare to them the appointed time of redemption and the consolation. Now, after the secret was revealed to him, it had been hidden from him; after the door had been opened to him, the door was closed to him. Our father Jacob replied and blessed them: He blessed each one according to his good works. ²[. . .] Our father Jacob replied and said to them: "Of Abraham, father of my father, is born the impure Ishmael as well as all the sons of Quetourah; and of Isaac, my father is born the impure Esau, my brother. And I, I am afraid that there be among you someone whose heart separates itself from his brothers in order to worship before foreign idols." The twelve tribes of Jacob replied in unison and said: *"Listen to us, Israel our Father!* YHWH our God, YHWH is one." Jacob replied and said: "Blessed be his name and also his royal glory for ever and ever!"

The theme of the secret revealed and then hidden (v. 1) shows the reaction of the Targum to the chronological speculation on the end of days and the time of the Messiah, common in apocalyptic milieux: this attitude can be compared to that of Jesus (cf. Mk. 13, 4 and 32). At the beginning of v. 2 a passage is omitted, for it simply repeats the end of v. 1. The end of this verse is completely transformed in order to introduce the profession of faith expressed in Dt. 6, 4, which has nothing in common with the primitive context. The law-giver said: "Listen, Israel . . ." The text says: "Listen, Israel our father . . ."

# 9

# THE WAITING FOR THE MESSIAH
## Tg. of Genesis 49, 8-12

In Hebrew Judah's blessing contains the announcement of a sovereignty that ultimately was to fall to an enigmatic personage: "the sceptre shall not stray from Judah nor the mace from between his feet until Shiloh comes whom the peoples shall obey." The Targum *Yerushalmi* does not concern itself with the historical interpretation of the text. But it profits from it to introduce an announcement of the Messiah.

> [8]"*Judah, your brethren shall praise you* and it is through your name that they shall be called Jews.[a] *Your hands shall take revenge upon your enemies,* all *the descendants of our father* shall be the first to hail *you.* [9]I compare you *Judah,* my son, to the *cub* of lions. You delivered Joseph my son from his murderers. Of the judgment of Tamar, my son, you are innocent. You shall lie down and you shall remain in the midst of battle *like the lion,* and *like the lioness,* and there shall be no people nor kingdom which can *hold up* against you. Kings *shall not be lacking* among[b] those of the house of *Judah,* nor scribes teaching the Law *among* the descendants of his descendants, *until* the King Messiah *comes* to whom the royalty belongs and to whom all kingdoms shall be subject.
> [11]How beautiful is the king Messiah who is to rise among those of the house of Judah! He *girds* his loins and goes forth to do battle against his foes, and he slaughters kings along with princes. He reddens the mountains with the blood of their slain and whitens the hills with the fat of their warriors. His garments drip with blood: he resembles a trampler of *grapes.*
> [12]How beautiful, the *eyes* of the king Messiah: more so than pure *wine!* For he does not make use of them either to look upon illicit carnal commerce or to shed innocent blood. *His teeth*

---

[a]A pun: Yehudah and Yehudayya.

[b]Kings and scribes constitute the framework of the nation. One presumed the permanence of a royal lineage up to the coming of the Messiah.

*are whiter than milk,* for he does not use them from that which
comes from acts of violence and pillagings. The mountains shall
be reddened with his wines and wine-presses. The hills *shall be
whitened* with an abundance of wheat and flocks of sheep and
goats.

Verses 11 and 12 constitute stanzas of a rhythmed poem which
celebrates first the warrior Messiah and then the pacific Messiah.
The connections with the Hebrew text are then reduced to a few
words that serve as supports to the symbols. The paraphrase of
v. 11 draws inspiration from Is. 63, 2-3, where it presumes the
messianic interpretation, which is absent today from the Targum
of Jonathan on Isaiah. The present text is one of the best witnesses to the Jewish doctrine of the Messiah, with his two-sided
face. But the New Testament preserves the image of the warrior
Messiah only in the images of Revelation (Rev. 19, 11-13).

The Targum of Onkelos, which is generally closer to the
Aramaic text of the original Hebrew, here amplifies it greatly.
While distancing itself from the Targum *Yerushalmi,* it likewise
introduces a messianic promise. It begins with the same play on
words on the name of Judah (Yehudah) and the verb "to praise"
(*hodah*):

> ⁸"Judah you are praise and not shame," *your brethren will
> praise you. Your hand* shall be *upon your enemies.* And your
> foes shall be shattered. They shall turn the nape of their necks
> before you and the descendants of your father shall be the first
> to hail you. ⁹He shall be prince from the beginning, and in the
> end there will be an Anointed among those of the house of
> Judah. For you have kept your soul distant from a sentence
> of death, my son. He shall lie down and shall remain mighty
> *like the lion and like the lioness.* There exists no kingdom that
> can shake him. ¹⁰Among those of the house *of Judah* shall not
> disappear a holder of power, nor scribes among the descendants
> of his descendants *until the Messiah comes* to whom the royalty
> shall belong and whom the peoples shall obey. ¹¹Israel shall sur-
> round his city; the people shall build his temple; the just shall
> be all around him and those who practice the Law shall instruct
> themselves with him. *His garment* shall be of a rich purple, and
> *his coat,* in fine wool tinged with scarlet and varied colors. ¹²His
> mountains shall be reddened with his vineyards, his vine-presses

overflow. His valleys shall be whitened with wheat and flocks of sheep and goats.

It is probable that the author of the Targum of Onkelos was familiar with the other targumic tradition whose main theme and several details he preserves. But he freely constructs his paraphrase, which was to become official in the synagogues.

# 10

# THE BLESSING OF JOSEPH
## Tg. of Genesis 49, 22-26

Most of the blessings given to the patriarchs are amplified in order to provide a meaning capable of edifying the Targum's listeners. To a great extent they revert to remembrance of sacred history. Along with that of Judah, just cited, Joseph's blessing is distinguished by its length. It is to be borne in mind that in the Jewish tradition at about the time of our era, Joseph was presented as a model of chastity. This theme recurs at the beginning of the Targum.

[22]Joseph, my son, you who have grown up, my son, you who have grown up, and have become powerful, you must become more powerful still. I compare you, Joseph my son, to a vine planted near the water springs, which thrusts its roots into the ground and passes through the cleft of rocks, which makes its branches rise toward the heights and surpasses all trees. It is thus that you, Joseph my son, surpass all the soothsayers of the Egyptians and all the wise men through your knowledge, when you were made to mount the second chariot of the Pharaoh and when they proclaimed before you: "Long live the Father of the king, who is master through knowledge and young in years!"

*The daughters* of kings and of princes espied you from the embrasures and listened to you from the windows, and they threw before you bracelets, rings, necklaces, brooches and all sorts of golden objects hopeful that you would raise your eyes and that you would look at one of them. Far from you, my son Joseph! You did not raise your eyes nor consider anyone of them [so as not to be associated with them in Gehenna in the world to come] (gl). The daughters of kings and of princes said to one another: "Such indeed is Joseph, the pious man who does not pursue the vision of his eyes and the thoughts of his heart, for it is they that make the son of man disappear from the world." That is why two tribes shall arise from you, Manasseh and Ephraim: they shall receive a share and an inheritance with their brethren in the division of the country. . . .

[23]All the soothsayers of the Egyptians and their sages spoke against him and could not get the better of him. They spoke ill of him before their lord, *they slandered him* before Pharaoh, king of Egypt, in order to cause him to fall from his high office and to remove him from his royal throne. In the palace of Pharaoh they spoke against him with a perfidious tongue which was more piercing against him than arrows. [24]*But he established* his trust *in the Mighty One.* He stretched forth his *hands* and his *arms* to implore mercy from the Mighty One of his father Jacob, him whose powerful arms guard all the tribes of *Israel.*

[25]May the Word of the *God of your father* come to your aid! *May* the God of heaven bless you with the best of the dew and of the rain that descend *from the heavens* above, and with the blessing of the springs of the abyss that rise from the earth *below!* Blessed be the *breasts* that you have suckled and the bowels in which you have reposed! [26]May the blessings of your father be added for you to the blessings with which my fathers, Abraham and Isaac, blessed me, those which the princes of the world, Esau and Ishmael coveted from the beginning! May all these blessings come and fashion a crown of honor *on the head of Joseph, on the forehead of the pious man* who was lord and prince in the country of Egypt, but who was caring of his father and of the glory of his *brethren.*

It is possible to point out in passing a parallel in Lk. 11, 27, namely the compliment addressed to the mother of Jesus (end of v. 26). Since this formula develops the Hebrew text which speaks of "blessings of breasts and bowels" in a very general way, we may infer that it is proper to the Targum of the passage whose oral tradition is anterior to the gospel text. All the texts amplify the primitive blessing by summarizing the principal episodes of the story of Joseph. This recourse to biblical narratives is one of the methods of the Targum. This one turns here toward the past, whereas the blessing of Judah was turned toward the future. The commentary becomes moralizing proposing Joseph as an example, in conformity with the sapiental dimension that characterized the biblical narratives from the beginning.

# 11

# THE ANNOUNCEMENT OF THE BIRTH OF MOSES
## Tg. of Exodus 1, 15-21

The Targum of Pseudo-Jonathan is alone in preserving the Pharaoh's premonitory dream which announces the birth of Moses and his predestined future. The dream serves to explain why the king orders the midwives to exterminate all male infants.

> Pharaoh said that while sleeping he had beheld, in a dream, the whole country of Egypt placed upon the scale of a balance and, on the other scale of the balance, a lamb, the young of an ewe. Now it was the scale on which the lamb was placed that lowered. Immediately he sent for all the magicians of Egypt and told them of his dream. Jannes and Jambres,[a] the heads of the magicians, immediately opened their mouths and told the Pharaoh: "A son is to be born in the gathering of Israel: thanks to him the whole country of Egypt is to be devastated." This is why Pharaoh, *the king of Egypt,* took counsel and said *to the Jewish mid-wives, one of whom was named Shiphrah—*

[a]See 2 Tim. 3, 8.

that is Jokabed—and the *second, Pu'ah*—that is Miriam her daughter[b]—[16]He said: *"When you shall assist the Jewish women in childbirth, you shall watch them* on the seat: if it is a male child, you shall kill it, *and if it is a girl, she shall live. But the mid-wives feared YHWH and they did not act as the king of Egypt had said: they let* the sons *live.*

To the king who reproached them, they replied:

[19]*"That is because the Jewish women are not like the Egyptian women.* They are alert and know what to do. *Before the mid-wife comes to them they raise* their eyes in prayer, beseeching and imploring mercy before their Father who is in the heavens. He listens to the voice of their prayers and they are immediately granted. *They* give birth and are *delivered without difficulty.* [20]*YHWH favored the mid-wives: the people became very numerous and very strong.* [21]*because the mid-wives had feared* YHWH they obtained a good renown for generations, and the Word of YHWH built for them the house of royalty and the house of sovereign priesthood.

Thus the Targum of Pseudo-Jonathan does not attribute only to Jokabed, the mother of Aaron and Moses, the privilege of being the ancestress of future high-priests. It also makes of Miriam, the sister of Moses, the ancestress of the Messiah. But the identification of the midwives, is without doubt relatively late.

[b]The identifications are peculiar to the Ps. -J.

# 12

# THE FOUR NIGHTS
## Tg. of Exodus 12, 41-42

The setting is that of the paschal night. The Targum profits from its mention in Scripture to introduce a poem that explains the meaning of this night as a memorial of the past and an announcement of the future.

⁴¹ "*At the end of the four hundred and thirty years, on this self-same day, all the armies of YHWH set forth,* liberated, from the country of Egypt. *It is a night of vigil,* prepared for the liberation in the name of YHWH, at the moment when he made the children of Israel, liberated, *leave the country of Egypt.*

⁴²Four nights are inscribed in the Book of the Memorials. The first night was when YHWH revealed himself over the world in order to create it. The world was without form and void and darkness extended over the face of the abyss,*ᵃ* and the Word of YHWH was Light and it shone. And he called it the first Night.

The second night was when YHWH appeared to Abraham, one hundred years old, and to Sarah ninety years old, in order to fulfill what Scripture states: "Is Abraham, one hundred years old, to beget, and Sarah, ninety years old, to give birth?*ᵇ* Now, Isaac was thirty-seven years old when he was offered upon the altar. The heavens stooped and descended and Isaac saw their totality. And he called it the second Night.

The third night was when YHWH appeared to the Egyptians in the middle of the night: his hand slew the first-born of the Egyptians and his right protected the first-born of Israel so that what Scripture states be fulfilled: "Israel is my first-born."*ᶜ* And he called it the third Night.

The fourth night, this will be when the world shall arrive at its end in order to be dissolved. The yokes of iron shall be smashed and the perverse generations annihilated. Moses shall arise from the middle of the desert and the king Messiah shall come out from above. The one shall advance at the head of the flock and the other shall advance at the head of the flock, and the word of YHWH shall advance between the two and they shall walk together.

*This is the night of the Passover* for the name of YHWH, *a night reserved* and fixed *for* the liberation of *all Israel down through the generations.*

As always when the Targum inserts a lengthy development, the end connects with the biblical text. On the second night, the men-

---

*ᵃ*Gen. 1, 2.

*ᵇ*Quotation from Gen. 17, 17.

*ᶜ*Ex. 4, 22.

tion of the birth of Isaac is there only in order to introduce the memory of his "binding" upon the pyre of sacrifice. The paschal night is at once the memorial of this sacrifice and of the departure from Egypt. To this two events in time are added: the creation (although the priestly calendar places the creation of the luminaries on the first day of Nisan and not on the fourteenth) and the great deliverance, evoked in a grandiose manner. To give this poem in full it is necessary to complete the text of Codex *Neofiti I* with that of the fragmentary Targum. There are several uncertainties in the translation. Instead of making the Messiah come from "above," one recension has him come from the "middle of Rome," and instead of having him walk with Moses "at the head of the flock," one text makes him advance "on a cloud" (cf. the Son of Man in Daniel 7). The essential fact is the meeting of the two liberators on the night of the eschatological Passover. The latter brings a definitive deliverance that liberates Israel from a wicked world of which Egypt was only the symbol. This theme was to be resumed and transformed by the Christian interpretation of Easter in which "Christ, our Passover, has been sacrificed" (1 Cor. 5, 7) as paschal lamb and as the new Isaac. Then will come the "new creation."

# 13

# ON THE ITINERARY OF THE EXODUS
## Tg. of Exodus 13, 17-18

A liturgical reading (*seder*) begins with Ex. 13, 17. It involves a notable amplification, in a recension of the fragmentary Tg. (Paris Ms. BN 110) and in Pseudo-Jonathan (TJ[1] or Ys.-J). Here the two sources are combined to give the legend in its entirety. It is based upon Ps. 78, 9 and 1 Chr. 7, 21. The error attributed to the Ephraimites stems from the difference between the four hundred years of Gen. 15, 13 and the 430 years of Ex. 12, 42.

The development is connected to the Tg. *Yerushalmi* on Ezek. 37 (see this text in 14, p. 44).

> [17]*It came to pass, when Pharaoh let go the people, that YHWH did not lead them along the road of the country of the Philistines, although it was nearest. For YHWH said: "I hope that the people not change their mind upon seeing* their brethren who died *in battle,* two hundred thousand valiant men of the tribe of Ephraim. Grabbing shields, spears and other weapons, they had gone down to Gath to pillage the flocks of the Philistines. But because they had transgressed the decision of the Word of YHWH by setting forth from Egypt thirty years before the appointed time, they were delivered into the hands of the Philistines who slaughtered them. These are the dried bones that the Word of YHWH made to live again through the mediation of Ezekiel in the valley of the Doura. [From the bones had been fashioned drinking vessels from which drank Nebuchadenezzar the impious. Now at the moment in which YHWH caused them to live again through the mediation of the prophet Ezekiel, they smote this impious one on the mouth. The bones joined with each other and lived again, and they rose to their feet, a very numerous army. They all arose, with the exception of one man who did not arise. The prophet said before YHWH: "What are the works of this only man who has not risen?" And YHWH said to him: he practiced lending against security and usury. This is why he shall not live again. It is thus that YHWH made Ezekiel see this sign, to show that he was to make the dead live again][a] If they had seen that, they would have been afraid and they *would have returned to Egypt:* [18]*YHWH therefore diverted the people along the road of the desert of the Sea of the Reeds* and each one with *five* little *children, the children of Israel went out from the country of Egypt* (TJ[1]).

The legend was formed to explain the change of the itinerary noted in the book of Exodus. It is probable that the text of Ex. 37 accompanied this liturgical reading. Hence the elaboration of its details. The mutual explanation of a text of the Law and of a text of the Prophets is a usual proceeding.

---

[a]The text between [ ] is found in the Paris Ms. BN 110 (Fragmentary Tg.).

# 14

# THE CROSSING OF THE RED SEA
## Tg. of Exodus 14, 11-16

The account of the crossing of the sea (Ex. 14) follows the biblical text, adding some details such as the interpretation of the place names (Pihahiroth, for example, becomes "the gambling den of licentiousness.") But in vv. 13–14, the dissection of the text into small pieces permits the introduction of a very developed narrative.

[11]*. . . They said to Moses: "Is it because there were no graves in Egypt that you have taken us away so as to cause us to perish in the desert? What have you done to us by bringing us out of Egypt?* [12]*Is this not what we told you in Egypt: leave us in the service of the Egyptians for it is better for us to serve the Egyptians than to perish in the desert?* [13]The children of Israel formed four parties when they stood on the shore of the Sea of Reeds. One was saying: "Let us hurl ourselves into the sea." Another was saying: "Let us go back to Egypt." Another was saying: "Let us form combat units against them." Another was saying: "Let us shout at them so as to sow confusion among them." To the party that was saying: *"Let us hurl ourselves into the sea," Moses said: "Fear not, but prepare yourselves to behold the deliverance that YHWH will accomplish for you today."* To the party that was saying: "Let us go back to Egypt," Moses said: *"Fear not, for the Egyptians that you see today, you will never see them again in servitude."* [14]To the party that was saying: "Let us form combat units," Moses said: "Fear not, it is YHWH who will make your *battles* victorious." To the party that was saying: "Let us shout at them so as to sow confusion among them," Moses said: "Fear not, be silent, render glory, praise and majesty to our God and exalt him." [15]YHWH said to Moses: "Up to how long will you stand there praying before me? Behold your prayer has been heard before me. As for the prayer of the children of Israel, it has preceded your own. *Speak to the children of Israel and let them set out.*

*¹⁶As for you, raise your hand over the sea, part it in two and the children of Israel will enter the sea dry shod."*

The different recensions of Tg. *Yerushalmi* are almost all to be found in this text. About all we can discover through it is the method of the targumist who makes the literalness of the Hebrew speak, by making of Moses' discourses a series of responses to the cries of anguished Israelites. This theme was already known from the *Book of Biblical Antiquities* (before 70 A.D. or C.E.) which, however, mentions only three parties. Thus the antiquity of the targumic tradition is also verified.

# 15

# SONG OF THANKSGIVING
## Tg. of Exodus 15, 1-18

The Song of Thanksgivings gathered in Ex. 15, 1-19, which develops Ex. 15, 21, is the subject of an amplification as is generally the case of psalms. To Codex *Neofiti I* (N) are added here its marginal glosses (gl), the fragmentary Targum (TJ²), the fragment G of the *Cairo Gueniza* and Pseudo-Jonathan, which fundamentally take up again the same themes by amplifying them. For each quotation the source followed is indicated.

> *¹Then Moses and the children of Israel sang this song of praises before YHWH and they said this:* Let us praise and glorify before YHWH, for he has extracted revenge from all those who had puffed up with pride before him: *horses and riders,* because they had puffed themselves up with pride and had pursued the people of the children of Israel, *he has hurled them* and drowned them in the Sea of Reeds (N). *²Our strength* and the greatness of our *praise,* is YHWH, dread of time without end. He has decided through his Word and *has made himself our* savior" (N). From the breasts of their mothers, the nurslings pointed

him out to their fathers[a] and said to them: "He is our father who made us suck the honey of the rock and anointed us with the oil drawn from the hard flint. (TJ² and gl). The children of Israel said: "*He* is our *God,* let us praise him, the God of our fathers, let us exalt him! (N) ³It is YHWH, in the glory of his presence who makes your *battles* victorious. In all the generations, he makes his might known to his people, the house of Israel (TJ²). As is his name, such is his might, such is his royalty. Blessed be his great *name* for ever through time without end! (Ms. 110)

⁹"Pharaoh the impious, the *enemy* and the adversary, said: "*I will* pursue the children of Israel and I will *overtake* them when they will be encamped on the shore of the sea. Among them, I will capture a great number and I will carry off a great booty from them. *I will distribute* the plunder among my people, my warriors, *until my soul is gorged with them.* After which, *I unsheath my sword and my right hand shall exterminate them.* ¹⁰*You blew through a wind* come before you, YHWH, and the waters *of the sea covered them over.* They sank and *they were swallowed up like lead in the mighty waters.* ¹¹*Who is your like among the gods* above, YHWH? *Who is your like, magnificent in holiness, formidable: in feats,* for time without end, working wonders and miracles for your people, the house of Israel? (N)

¹²The sea and the land disputed with each other. The sea said to the land: "Receive your children!" But the land told the sea: "Receive your victims!" The sea did not want to receive them and the land did not want to swallow them. The land feared the judgment of the great day. But through a word before you, *you stretched forth your right hand* with an oath and you swore to the earth that you would not lay claim to them in the world to come. *Thereupon* the land opened its mouth and *swallowed them.* (TJ²)

¹⁸When the children of Israel saw the signs and the wonders that the Holy One—Blessed be He!—had wrought for them on the shore of the sea—Blessed be his great name forever in the world without end!—they rendered glory, praise and exultation to their God. The children of Israel took the Word and said to one another: "Come, let us set the crown upon the head of

[a]Cf. Wis. 10, 21.

the Liberator, for he makes pass away and does not pass away, he makes change and does not change. He is the king of kings in this world below, and it is to him that belongs the crown of royalty for the world to come and it belongs to him for ever in the world without end.''

In v. 2 the gloss draws its inspiration from the song of Moses in Deuteronomy (Dt. 32, 13; see this text). The tradition that it gathers might have inspired Wis. 10, 21. Verse 12 is notable for the dispute between the land and the sea. The final verse (v. 18) amplifies the theme of divine royalty: ''YHWH shall reign always and forever.'' Here we see that the Targum, by amplifying the biblical texts, continues the fundamental themes of the Jewish faith.

# 16

# THE DECALOG
## Tg. of Exodus 20, 1-17

The setting of Ex. 19 and 20, 18-21 is slightly amplified in the Targum *Yerushalmi* in all its forms. Here we follow the text of the *Cairo Gueniza* (Fragment F of the P. Kahle collection).

>¹And the Word of YHWH pronounced all the magnificence of his commandments, saying: ²The first commandment when it issued forth from the mouth of the Holy One—Blessed be his name!—was like sparks, lightning flashes and lamps of fire, a lamp of fire to his right and a lamp of fire to his left. It flew and whirled in the air of the heavens. All Israel beheld it and was afraid because of it. Then it came back and engraved itself on the two tablets of the covenant. It cried out then and said to the children of Israel: ''My people, children of Israel, I am YHWH, *your God who* liberated and *brought you out,* ransomed, *from the country of Egypt,* from the house of bondage of slaves.''

> ³The second commandment, when it issued forth from the mouth of the Holy One—blessed be He—was like sparks. . . .

The same setting is resumed a second time. We can presume that in the oral tradition it preceded each commandment. It is not to be forgotten that in the Jewish tradition, the gift of the commandments at the time of the covenant on Sinai, is fixed chronologically on the day of Pentecost. The scene in the Acts of the Apostles (Acts 2) uses the same imagery of tongues of fire, but there is a substitution of the gift of the Spirit for that of the commandments.

> ". . . He cried out then and said: "My people, house of Israel, you shall have no other God besides me. 'You *shall not make a statue, nor a sculpture nor any image whatsoever of what there is in the heavens above, nor of what there is in the earth below, nor of what there is in the waters beneath the earth.* You *shall not bow down before them and you shall not worship before them, for I,* YHWH, your God, I am a jealous and vindictive God, who takes revenge with jealousy, who recalls the faults of sinful fathers *upon* the rebel descendants up to the *third* and *up to the fourth generation of* those who hate me, ⁶*but* who keeps the covenant and benevolence *up to thousands* of generations *for my friends* the just and *for those who keep the commandments* of my law."

Respect for the name of God (v. 6) is the subject of slight additions, except in the Paris Ms. (BN 110) which adds:

> . . . For I, YHWH your great God, I am the avenger who will take revenge upon anyone who lies by my name. For it is by my great name that the world was created, and whoever swears falsely by my name, it is clear before me that I will destroy him for his faults. But whoever keeps his soul and does not swear falsely, it is clear before me that the world endures thanks to him, and all those thanks to whom the world endures shall have happiness in this world and in the world to come . . .

Likewise the commandment of the Sabbath (v. 8), slightly amplified by all the texts, receives an interesting addition in the Paris Ms. (BN 110).

. . . It is the first of festivals, the most solemn of the festal days and the most desirable, because for the children of Israel its solemnity stems from its Law, and whoever honors the Sabbath is comparable before me to the one who honors me on my throne of glory. For it is on account of the honor of the Sabbath that the children of Israel shall inherit the world to come which is all sabbath.

The commandment of the honor due to the father and the mother (v. 12) is commented on in the same way by Ms. BN 110. But the six following commandments are the subject of an amplification of a different style:

> [13]My people, children of Israel, be not murderers, nor companions of murderers. Let one not see in the gathering of Israel a people of murderers lest your descendants be raised like you and be habituated to being with murderers. For it is on account of the sins of the murderers that the sword comes down upon the world.
>
> [14]My people, children of Israel, be not adulterers, nor companions nor accomplices of adulterers. Let one not see in the gathering of Israel a people of adulterers, lest your descendants be raised like you and learn only to be adulterers. For it is on account of the sins of adulterers that the plague descends upon the world.

The same formulary is found with thieves (v. 15), for it is on account of them that famine descends upon the world; with those who bear false witness (v. 16), for it is on account of them that drought descends upon the world; with the covetous (v. 17), for it is on account of them that captivity is present in the world. We see that the transformation of the biblical text attempts to give more warmth to the formularies and to make precise the sanctions related to them. Again we find the same amplifications, with the exception of a few details, in the version of Deuteronomy (Dt. 5, 6-21). The different recensions of the Tg. *Yerushalmi* present only secondary variants. All this is explained when we recall that this text was intended to be a solemn liturgical reading. This is why the text is found again in the *Mazhor Vitry* (medieval collection).

# 17

# THE REMEMBRANCE OF
# THE THREE PATRIARCHS
## Tg. of Leviticus 22, 26-27

In the very middle of the law on sacrificial animals (Lev. 22, 17–30), the mention of the calf, the lamb and the kid leads the targumist to evoke the memory of the three patriarchs (22, 27). In order to do this he invokes the remembrance of the three passages of Genesis that mention the animals. The reading of Lev. 22, 26–23, 24 was a paschal reading. It is not to be forgotten that the three texts of Genesis were also connected with the festival of Passover. This coincidence explains a comparison that otherwise would appear artificial.

> [26]YHWH *spoke to Moses saying:* . . . [27]There was a time when you recalled in our favor the order of our offerings that we offered before you, one year after the other, and our offerings constituted for us the expiation for our faults. But now that the faults have produced their effect, we no longer have aught to offer from our flocks of live-stock.
>
> The bull was chosen before me at first, in order to recall the Ancient of the East[a] perfectly pure. He offered a calf in your name. He ran to the flock, took a tender and fat calf, gave it to his servant, and his servant hastened to prepare it. He had unleavened loaves of bread baked and gave the angels to eat, and he merited to see himself apprised that Sarah would give birth to Isaac.
>
> The lamb was chosen in the second place to recall the merit of the Just[b] who himself bound himself upon the altar and extended his neck for the sake of your name, YHWH. The heavens lowered and descended and Isaac beheld the totality thereof and his eyes dimmed on account of the heights. This is why he merited that a lamb be prepared in his stead for the holocaust.

[a]Abraham.
[b]Isaac.

And there is a kid in the third place, to recall the merit of the Perfect[c] who clothed himself in kid's skins and prepared viands which he brought to his father. He made his father eat of these viands, he made him drink wine and merited to receive the series of the blessings from Isaac, his father, and to give rise to twelve holy tribes for the sake of your name.

This is why Moses, the prophet of YHWH, explains and says "My people, children of Israel!" *(Gueniza) When a calf, a lamb or a kid will be born, it shall be raised for seven days by its mother, then from the eighth day and beyond, it will be fit for* the offering before YHWH. (N)

A word suffices to give rise to a reminiscence of Genesis. The very remembrance of the three patriarchs is essential to the Jewish faith. There is the Ancient, the Just, and the Perfect. The remembrance of Isaac on the pyre, already recalled in the "Poem on the Four Nights" (on Ex. 12, 42), will occasionally recur in the Targum of Isaiah (Tg. Is. 33, 7-9, p. 82). It is here that Isaac's blindness is best explained. Earlier we omitted the texts that relate the apparition to Abraham of three mysterious personages, whom the Tg. here calls angels, to Isaac's blessing of Jacob. It is clear that the usurping of the paternal blessing, in which Jacob benefits, in no way disconcerts the targumist. He would willingly cite the words of St. Augustine: Jacob clothed in kid's skin "is not a lie, it is a mystery." But the "mystery" is interpreted in a specifically Jewish way. The introduction of the targumic development explores a problem of conscience posed by the destruction of the Temple and the end of the sacrificial cult. The recension cited is from a manuscript of the *Cairo Gueniza* and from the fragmentary Targum (TJ²). But the end is borrowed from the Codex *Neofiti I,* so as to provide the complete text.

[c] Jacob.

# 18

# THE FOUR JUDGMENTS OF MOSES
## Tg. of Leviticus 24, 10-14

A case of blasphemy provides the occasion for a rule of jurisprudence so as to state precisely the punishment due to the blasphemer. The Targum *Yerushalmi* in all its preserved forms introduces a *halaka* (a law or ordinance not written in the Scriptures but based upon an oral interpretation of them) relative to judgments. This same development is found again in four places (cf. Tg. of Num. 9, 8; 15, 34; 27, 5). It preposes the principle of swift judgment in regard to goods, and temporization in regard to capital cases.

> [10]*The son of an Israelite woman, who was also the son of an Egyptian man, went out (. . .) among the children of Israel. The son of the Israelite* woman *quarreled with an Israelite man in the camp.* [11]*Now the son of the Israelite woman* pronounced the holy *Name* with imprecations and blasphemed it. *He was brouht before Moses. The name of the woman was Shalomit, dauhter of Dibri, of the tribe* of the children of *Dan.*
>
> [12]It is one of the four cases that were brought before Moses and he decided upon them with the agreement of on high. In two among them Moses was swift and in two of them Moses was slow. In all four, he said: "I have not understood." In regard to the impure who were unable to observe Passover (Num. 9, 8) and the daughters of Selofkhad (Num. 27, 5), Moses was swift because their cases were of a pecuniary order. In the matter of him who had deliberately profaned the sabbath by gathering wood (Num. 27, 5), and in the matter of the blasphemer who had pronounced the holy Name with imprecations, Moses was slow because their cases were capital matters. It was in order to teach judges to be swift in pecuniary cases and slow in capital cases, so they not pass a hasty death sentence upon the one who is worthy of a death by trial, for the case in which, during the trial, other proofs might be found for his release, and so that they would not be ashamed to say: "We have not under-

stood," since Moses their master had said: "I have not understood."

*Therefore one was locked in prison* until what judgment was
to be applied to him *was decided* by YHWH. *[13] Then YHWH
spoke to Moses saying: [14] "Let him who blasphemed leave the
camp. Those who have understood shall lay their hands upon
his head and all the people of the community shall stone him."*

The end of the text (vv. 15–16) takes up the text of the biblical
law with very slight additions. We see that the additional *halaka*
is a juridical precision brought to already fixed points of law:
jurisprudence completes the written law and its transmission
through the Targum shows the universality of its application. This
poses a problem in regard to the trial of Jesus related in the
Gospels. It was a capital case. In her studies of the chronology
of the Supper and of the Passion, A. Jaubert has argued on the
basis of this text for support of her hypothesis, according to which
the Supper took place on Tuesday evening and sentence was
delayed in order to postpone the delivery of Jesus to Pilate until
Friday (*Revue de l'Histoire des Religions* 167 [1965] 26–30). It
is a topic of discussion among historians.


# 19

# THE PROPHECY OF
# ELDAD AND MEDAD
# Tg. of Numbers 11, 26


In Num. 11 the story of the quails is interrupted by a narrative
in which Moses assembles seventy elders—sages, says the
Targum—and the Spirit descends and rests upon them. This is
the context of the episode of the two men among those who prophesied "in the camp":

> *[26] Two men had remained in the camp. The name of one was
> Eldad and the name of the other was Medad. And the Holy*

*Spirit rested upon them.* Eldad prophesied and said: "Behold
quails are going to rise from the sea and they shall be a
stumbling-block for Israel." And Medad prophesied and said:
"Behold Moses the prophet is to be removed from the middle
of the camp and Joshua, son of Nun, will occupy after him
his office of leader." And both prophesied together saying: "At
the extreme end of days, Gog and Magog shall rise against
Jerusalem and fall by the hands of the king Messiah. And during seven years the children of Israel shall make fire with their
weapons without going out into the thickets." *Now they were
part of the seventy sages* who had been set apart, and the seventy sages *did not leave* the camp as long as Eldad and Medad
*prophesied in the camp.*

As in the biblical text, Moses then wanted all the people to receive the Spirit of prophecy in the same way. The subjects of the
prophetic proclamations are deserving of note. They concern at
first the sequel of the story as the biblical account relates it. But
in order to complete the account they turn toward "the end of
days": the battle of the Messiah against Gog and Magog is a classic theme which was to be taken up in the New Testament (Rev.
20, 8), by way of a transposition that was to substitute the Church
for the people of Israel. The prophecy relating to the succession
of Moses is ancient: it was already cited in the *Book of Biblical
Antiquities* 20, 5 (before the year 70 A.D. or C.E.).


# 20

# THE BRONZE SERPENT
## Tg. of Numbers 21, 4-9


⁴. . . *On the way, the soul of the people was afflicted.*⁵ The
people spoke counter to the Word of YHWH and they murmured *against Moses:* "*Why did you bring us out of Egypt so
as to make us die in the desert? For we have neither bread* to
eat *nor water* to drink and *our soul is weary of this* bread which

is *a scanty nourishment.* " [6]An echo[a] came forth from the earth and its voice made itself heard up to the very heights: "Come see, all creatures! come listen, all sons of the flesh. Formerly I damned the serpent and said to it: "Dust shall be your nourishment.[b] Now, I have had my people brought out of the country of Egypt and made the manna of heaven come down for them. I made the well gush forth from the abyss for them and transported quails for them from the sea. And my people has again begun to murmur before me about the manna assertedly of scant worth. Let come the serpent, who did not murmur on account of his nourishment, and let it rule over the people that has murmured on account of its nourishment. This is why YHWH *sent the fiery serpents against the people. They bit the people and a great number of the people of Israel died.* [7]*The people came to Moses and they said: "We have sinned for we have spoken* against the Word of YHWH and murmured *against you.* Pray before YHWH *so that he drive the serpents away from us.* "

Moses thereupon makes the bronze serpent, and the fragmentary Tg. (TJ²) concludes:

> [9]. . . he laid it upon a high place. And it came to pass that whoever was bitten by a serpent lifted his face in prayer toward his Father who is in the heavens and *turned his gaze toward the bronze serpent,* and he lived.

The comparison between the plague of the serpents and the serpent of Genesis is obvious. But it requires a great deal of imagination to justify detailed comparisons in regard to the murmurings. The echo, here as in other places, is literally a "daughter of the voice," but this time it does not come from heaven. The enumeration of God's benefactions mentions the well, soon to be discussed. Let us note at the end of the text the classical expression of Jewish prayer: God is "the Father who is in the heavens."

[a]Lit. "daughter of the voice."
[b]Cf. Gen. 3, 14.

# 21

# THE METAMORPHOSIS
# OF AN ITINERARY
## Tg. of Numbers 21, 13-20

[13]In Hebrew the text glossed is a fragment of an itinerary interrupted by two poetic quotations. The Hebrew text is here given first so that the puns that lie at the foundation of the haggadic development can be seen.

> [13]They set out from there and camped beyond the torrent of Arnon . . . This torrent rose, in the desert, from the country of the Amorites. For the Arnon was on the frontier of Moab, between the Moabites and the Amorites. [14]This is why it is written in the Book of the Wars of YHWH: [15]Waheb near Suphah and the torrent of Arnon, and the slope that slants toward the site of Ar and leans on the frontier of Moab. [16]. . . And from there they went to Beer[a] . . . It was in regard to this well that YHWH had said to Moses: "Gather the people and I will give them water." [17]Then it was that Israel sang this song: "Of the well, sing!" [18]The well was dug by the leaders of the people with the sceptre, with their staves." . . . And from Beer to Mattana;[b] [19]from Mattana to Nahaliel;[c] from Nahaliel to Bamot;[d] and from Bamot to the valley that expands into the open field of Moab, toward the height of Pisgah which rises opposite the desert.[e]

This itinerary is transformed into accounts that accentuate the interpretation of place names and end with the story of the well that followed the Israelites in their desert crossing:

---

[a]Beer = well.
[b]Root of Natam = to give.
[c]Torrent of God.
[d]Heights.
[e]Yeshimon = desert.

[13]*They left from there and camped beyond the Arnon which is in the desert and rises from the frontiers* of the Amorites. *For the Arnon is the frontier of the Moabites, between the Moabites and the Amorites.* [14]*This is why they are* written and explained in the book of the Law of YHWH, which is comparable to the *book of Wars,* the marvels that YHWH performed for Israel when it stood near the Sea of Reeds, and the great feats that he wrought for them when they crossed *the torrents of the Arnon.* [15]As the children of Israel were crossing the torrents of the Arnon, the Amorites had hidden in caves of the torrents of the Arnon, saying to themselves: "When the children of Israel will cross, we shall rush out at them and we will slay them." But the Master of all things, YHWH, made a sign, he who knows what is in hearts and before whom it is clear what there is in the loins; he made a sign to the mountains, and they brought their summits together, one with the other, and crushed the heads of their valorous men, and *the torrents overflowed with their blood.* But they (= the Israelites) did not know of the marvels and of the great feat that YHWH had wrought for them in the torrents. After that they (= the mountains) separated and return to their places. Lahhayyat*ⁿ* (= Ar-Moab), the city small fort that was not in their plan, was saved. Behold it is near *the frontier of the Moabites.* [16]*And from there the well* was given to them. It is in regard to this well that YHWH had said to Moses: *"Gather the people and I will give them water."* [17]Then Israel sang this song of praises: "Rise up, well," *they sang* to it. And it rose up. [18]The well *that had been dug* formerly by *the princes* of the world, Abraham, Isaac, and Jacob, the circumspect men of the people finished it, the seventy sages who had been set apart; the masters of Israel, Moses and Aaron, measured it with *their staves,* and from the desert it was *given as a gift* (= Mattana) to them. [19]And after being given to them as a gift, the well changed for them into raging *torrents* (= Nahaliel), and after becoming raging torrents, it began to rise *to the top* (= Bamot) of the mountains and to descend with them into the deep *valleys.* [20]And after rising with them on the tops of the mountains and after descending with them in the deep valleys, it was hidden from them *in the valley*

---

*ⁿ*Litt.: the small fort.

*that opens* on the frontier of the *Moabites,* at the top of the
*height that looks in the direction of Beth-Jeshimon.*

It is clear that the transformation of the text is total. The account developed on v. 15 begins from the mention of the torrent
and explains that there were torrents of blood in that spot. The
two proper names are passed over in silence. In v. 16, the mention of Beer introduces the theme of the well given in the desert
to give water to Israel. Other passages explain that it is the well
of Miriam, obtained by her personal merits. But finally it is associated with the water that flows from the rock (Num. 20, 1-11).
The puns in vv. 18 and 19 on the proper names of the itinerary
are able to present the well as journeying with the Israelites. From
the Targum comes the rabbinic legend of the rock that follows
Israel in the desert in order to give Israel the necessary water, a
legend known in the *Book of Biblical Antiquities* and cited by
St. Paul (1 Cor. 10, 3). Here we can verify the antiquity of the
targumic tradition, since the legend could not have come into
being save through the interpretation of the proper names that
form the itinerary described in the biblical text. But the desert
well is further identified with the wells discussed in the story of
the patriarchs (v. 18). Thus the patriarchs are recalled in the context of the desert episode. The internal connections of Scripture
are thus assured.

# 22

# THE ORACLES OF BALAAM
## Excerpts from Numbers 23–24

Like Jacob's blessings at the end of Genesis, Balaam's oracles
lend themselves to amplifications regarding Israel's future until
the eschatological end. The remembrance of the patriarchs and
of their wives (23, 9) introduces praise of the people of God, while
the "prophet despite himself" announces that he will have "no

share in the world come" (23, 10). The following oracle (23, 18-29) praises Israelite monotheism (become the monotheism of the Targumist):

> (23) *"Behold* I have been brought hither in order to *bless."* *I will bless Israel* and *I will not refuse* the blessing. [21]I *do not see* servants *of the life among* those of the house of *Jacob* nor servants of the worship of idols *among* those of the house of *Israel.* The word of YHWH their God is with them and the brightness of the glory of their King is a shield *above them.* [22]*God brought them out* of Egypt, he *whose is* the power, the praise and the majesty. [23]*For* I do not see augurs among those of the house of *Jacob, nor* soothsayers *among* those of the house of Israel. *At that time, one shall announce* to the house of *Jacob* the good things and the consolations that are to befall you, as also to those of the house of *Israel."* Balaam then declaimed in his prophetic poem: "Happy you the just! What good reward is prepared for you from YHWH in the world to come!
> . . .

The end of the oracle announces that Israel will not rest before putting its enemies to death. The hope of eternal reward (compare Mt. 5, 12 and Lk. 6, 23) does not therefore lessen the rigor of an aggressive nationalism.

The third oracle (24, 5-9) joins the praise of the tents of Jacob to that of the "Tent of Meeting," which is the sign of the presence of God in the midst of his people (v. 5). The Hebrew text said subsequently: "Water drips from its buckets, its seed has abundant waters, its king is greater than Agag and its kingdom is exalted" (v. 7). The targumist's thought then turns toward the messianic kindom:

> [24]"Their king shall rise among them and their liberator shall be one among them. He will gather their deported from the provinces of their adversaries and his descendants will have dominion over numerous peoples. He shall be mightier than Saul who forgave Agag, king of the Amalekites, and the kingdom of the king Messiah shall be exalted."

After this evocation, it is not surprising to come upon a profoundly nationalist evocation of victory (v. 8-9).

The last oracle which is made up of several fragments (24, 17-24) denotes the same atmosphere. It was already present in the Hebrew text in connection with the Star that arises from Jacob and the Sceptre that arises from Israel. Here the revenge against the nation's enemies is actualized in terms of the problems of the moment, in the wake of the destruction of Jerusalem and the failure of the second Jewish revolt:

> (24) [17]I see it, but it is not now; I observe it but it is not near. A king is to rise among those of the house of Jacob, a leader among those of the house of Israel. He will slaughter the strong men of the Moabites, he will exterminate all the descendants of Seth and he will strip the holders of riches.[18] Edom will become a dependency; the mountain of Gebal, a dependency for his enemies, and Israel will prosper in multiple riches. [19]A king is to rise among those of the house of Jacob and he will exterminate whoever shall be guilty in the guilty city, namely Rome
> . . .

Pseudo-Jonathan is even more precise:

> "A leader shall rise among those of the house of Jacob, he shall make perish the survivors of Constantinople, who will endure, the sinner city, Rome, and Caesarea, the strength of the city of nations."

The first text came from the Codex *Neofiti I,* completed by the fragmentary Targum, where a Christian censor had scratched out the name of Rome. But the same operation was performed on the text of the Pseudo-Jonathan: the censorship looked over the shoulder of the copyist who, however, was working for Christian readers.

The end of the oracle evokes the struggle against Gog and Magog (v. 20), the impregnable character of the fortress of Petra (v. 21-22), and an end of days in which the prophecy of the annihilation of Rome reappears.

> [23]Ah! Who will live in those days when the wrath of YHWH will be kindled to punish the impious and give to the just their rewards, and when he will hurl the kingdoms against each other? [24]Numerous multitudes shall depart in galleys from the province of Italy, that is to say of Rome. To them shall be added

numerous legions coming from the Romans. *They shall sub-jugate the Assyrians* and shall oppress all the descendants of Trans-Euphrates. But the end of the one and the other *shall be annihilation* and their destruction will last forever.

There is here an historical allusion to the battles between Romans and Parthians on the Euphrates, which has already appeared in the Revelation of John (Rev. 9, 14). But what counts is the end: the reward of the just of Israel and the global annihilation of the other nations. The possible existence of just persons in these nations is not even envisaged. Religious nationalism is total.

# 23

# INTRODUCTION TO DEUTERONOMY
## Tg. of Deuteronomy 1, 1-2

The Hebrew text of Deuteronomy begins with a journey. The Targum uses the place names in the Hebrew text as the foundation of its transformation of the text into an evocation of God's gifts and of Israel's rebellion.

> [1] *These are the words that Moses addressed to all the children of Israel.* He admonished them when they were beyond the Jordan. Moses began to speak and said to them: "Was not the Law given to you *in the desert* and on the mountain of Sinai, then explained to you *on the plains of Moab*? What signs YHWH has fulfilled with you, children of Israel! When you stood on the shore of the Sea *of Reeds,*[a] the sea was divided before you and became twelve roads, a road for each tribe. At sea you provoked his wrath and you rebelled[b] on the shore of the Sea of Reeds. On account of explorers that you had sent

[a] = Suph.
[b] Play on words on Tophel.

from the desert of *Paran* to reconnoiter the country of Canaan, he decreed upon you that you would not enter into the country of Israel. Then on account of the manna of which you said: 'Our soul is disgusted with this bread which is a scant nourishment,' he let loose serpents against you, at *Haceroth,* your dead bodies fell on account of the meat that you coveted. On account of the golden calf[c] which you made, YHWH decided through his Word to exterminate you. But because he remembered in your favor the covenant that he had contracted with your fathers, Abraham, Isaac and Jacob, of the Tent of Meeting that you made for his name and of the ark of the covenant of YHWH which you introduced therein by covering it with pure gold, he decided through his Word to forgive you your faults.''

The text continues by glossing Deuteronomy in order to explain that instead of taking the eleven days required to make the journey from Sinai to Cades, the Israelites took forty years (v. 2). The tonality of the Targum is thus indicated from its very first page. It reinforces that of Deuteronomy. To establish the text requires that Codex *Neofiti I,* deficient on several points, be completed by its marginal glosses and the fragmentary Tg. (TJ[2]). Beyond the punishments evoked, the reason that prompted God to forgive them, was retained: namely, the covenant given to the patriarchs and the promises linked to it. Compare Gal. 3, 17-18.

[c]In Hebrew, *Zahab* = "gold," play on words on the name of the place "Dizahab."

# 24

# THE CURSES OF MOSES
## Tg. of Deuteronomy 28, 15

Chapter 28 of Deuteronomy contains the series of blessings and announcements of calamities that bring the statute-book of Deuteronomy to a close. At the beginning of the announcement of calamity or curses, the Targum of Pseudo-Jonathan interpolates an appropriate scenario:

> [15]When Moses the prophet began to pronounce these words of reproach, the earth shook, the heavens trembled, the sun and the moon darkened and the stars lost their brightness.[a] The patriarchs cried out from their graves, when all the creatures were hushed and the trees kept their foliage still. The patriarch bean to speak and said: "Woe unto our descendants when, after having sinned, these curses shall come down upon them. How will they be able to endure them? Perhaps they will be struck with extermination and our merit will be unable to protect them, and there will be no man who rises to present petitions in their favor." An echo fell from the height of the heavens and said thus: "Fear not, O patriarchs. For even if the merit of all the generations should come to be lacking, your truth will never be lacking and the covenant that I have contracted with you shall never be abolished: it will protect them." And Moses the prophet began to speak and said: "Though I address reproaches to them, it is conditionally that they are threatened in these terms: If you *do not obey* the Word of YHWH your *God* by not vigilantly attending *to the practice of all his commandments and all his laws, that I prescribe for you today, all the curses shall come down upon you and overtake you.*"

It is a matter of not making the curses absolutes which would destroy Israel's hope. No doubt obedience is indicated as the basic condition for escaping them. But there is no need to fear that they will lead to Israel's extermination, for the merits of the patriarchs outweigh the sins of subsequent generations and ensure God's mercy. Here is one of the fundamental points of Jewish hope. In the Christian order of things the patriarchs remain only an example of faith in the promises, and their merits are superseded by the merits of Christ.

[a]Compare Mt. 24, 29 and 27, 45, 51.

# 25

# THE SONG OF MOSES
## Tg. of Deuteronomy 32

The Song of Moses, like all the biblical songs, lends itself to amplifications. We cannot quote it here in its entirety, but already its introduction is instructive, since a lengthy text precedes the first sentence:

> "When the time came for Moses the prophet to be withdrawn
> in peace from amid the world, Moses thought in his heart and
> said to himself: "Woe to me now, because I am to be with-
> drawn from the world and I have not yet borne witness to the
> sons of the Lord.[a] If I take as witness sons of men who die and
> taste the cup of death[b] the people will die and their decisions
> will be annulled. I am going to take as witness the heaven and
> the earth that never die and do not taste the cup of death, but
> whose end is to be consumed in the world to come." Thus did
> Isaiah the prophet explain and say: "Raise your eyes toward
> the *heavens* and gaze upon the *earth* below, for the heavens will
> vanish like smoke and the earth wear out like a garment.[c] "But
> YHWH is going to "create new *heavens* and a new *earth.*[d] In-
> deed two prophets have arisen to bear witness against Israel:
> Moses the prophet and Isaiah the prophet. Moses, because he
> was near the heavens and withdrawn from the earth, said to
> the *heavens:* "Give ear" and to the *earth:* "Listen." And both,
> because they feared the Holy Name, rose up to bear witness
> against Israel. It was thus that Moses, the prophet of YHWH
> arose. He mustered up courage and said: *"Give ear, heavens,
> and I will speak and may the earth hearken to the words from
> my mouth."*

[a]We have here the Greek word Kyrios.

[b]Compare Mk. 10, 38 and 14, 36.

[c]Is. 51, 6, in another Targum than that of Jonathan.

[d]Is. 65, 17.

After v. 2, which praises Moses' words, we find a curious numerical speculation:

> ³Moses the prophet said to the impious: Woe to the impious who recall the Holy Name by blaspheming, when it is not even possible for a single one of the angels in attendance to recall the holy Name before those of Israel who say: "holy, holy, holy," three times. It is from them that Moses learned not to recall the holy name until he had initiated his mouth by twenty one words that form twenty-five letters. It is thus that he explains and says: (The twenty-one first words of the song of Moses follow in Hebrew). This is why Moses the prophet said: "*For it is by the holy* Name *that* I pray, and you, my people, children of Israel, *render glory* and praise and *exaltation* to your God."

The text establishes a comparison between the beginning of the song of Moses and that of the book of Isaiah. The targumist remarks that the heavens and the earth are not cited in the same order in the two texts and he justifies this difference by utilizing two quotations from Isaiah that do not coincide with the Tg. of Jonathan on the prophet. But it is a matter of justifying the prophecy pronounced against Israel. Verse 3 has recourse to a very artificial procedure: it counts the letters contained in the prophecy (in Hebrew). It is also a matter of justifying recourse to the name of the Holy One: this it does by citing the Song of Is. 6. The end of the development rejoins the biblical text, slightly glossed in v. 2. Verse 4 presents the action of God in his constant providence:

> ⁴Moses the prophet said: "I have seen the master of the world without end, YHWH, dividing the day and making four parts thereof: three hours to pore over the Law; three hours to sit in judgment; three hours to assemble the couples between man and woman, elevating the one, lowering the others; three hours to govern the world. He is the Just before whom there is no lie, *for all his ways are justice and truth,* he is the *faithful* God before whom there is no iniquity."

Verses 5–8 add only slight commentaries. But vv. 10–13 largely amplify the text:

> [10]*He met them* dwelling *in the steppe* and in the *hubbub of
> the desert.* For forty years he guided them in the desert. He
> caused the manna of heaven to come down for them. He made
> the well spring up for them and led quails from the sea to them.
> He made the glory of his Presence dwell all around them. He
> taught them the ten words. He *protected* and watched over them
> like the eyelid protects the pupil of the eye. [11]*Like the vulture
> that awakens its nest and hovers over its young.* It spreads its
> wings and bears them on its powerful plumage . . . (v. 12).
> [13]He made them ride upon the heights of the country and made
> them eat the yield of royal delights: he made them suck the
> honey from the rock and anointed them *with the oil coming
> from the hard stone of flint.*

The enumeration of God's gifts summarizes the benefactions
of the exodus and of the desert crossing. For the end of the text,
we shall compare the Tg. of Ex. 15, 2, which utilizes this text.
The meditation on the blessings of the exodus nourishes Israel's
piety unceasingly. At the end of the passage one notes a text utilized in the haggadic development of 15, 1. In that which precedes, v. 1 merely develops the biblical text by comparing Moses
and Isaiah in two parallel biblical passages. Verse 3 gratuitously
introduces an announcement of the calamity about to befall the
impious by speculating on the beginning of the song in Hebrew
(twenty-one words of eighty-five letters). For the enumeration of
Israel's blessings in v. 10, compare 1 Cor. 10, 1-4. The continuation enumerates Israel's acts of ingratitude by expanding the biblical text. This is why the targumist enumerates, in turn, the
calamities to come by historicising them. The Hebraic text said:

> [23]I will heap calamities upon them, I will exhaust my arrows
> against them. [24]I will have granaries of famine for weapons,
> fever and consumption for poison. I will send against them the
> fang of wild beasts with the venom of reptiles.

Pseudo-Jonathan, which is the most developed of the Targums
on this point, glosses as follows:

**Ps J on Dt. 32, 23-24**
[23]When they will be in Babylon, they will worship their idols.
This is why I have decided through my Word to heap up
calamities upon them: *I will exhaust against them the arrows*

*of my vengeance.* ²⁴From the place of captivity of Babylon, I
will exile them to Media and to Elam. Those of the house of
Agag shall oppress them, those who are comparable to
demons*e* swollen with *hunger* and to the spirit of ruins
*devoured* by birds and to the demons of noon inhabited by ill
winds and to the demons of the night puffed up by ill winds.
*I will hurl against them* the Greeks who bite heartily like the
*wild beasts* and I will exile them by means of the Idumaeans*f*
who are full of *poison* like venomous serpents, the *reptiles* of
the earth.

The fragmentary Tg. is more succinct, but it introduces an allusion to the four kingdoms:

> ²³I have said through my Word that *I would have come upon
> them* disasters: *arrows,* signs of my punishments that I will hurl
> against them. ²⁴Beasts of *famine* and of plagues of locusts pos-
> sessed by evil spirits, and the teeth of the four kingdoms that
> are comparable to wild beasts.

This is only a fraction of the announcement of the punishments
promised to Israel, those that end with the perspective of Gehenna (v. 35). Toward the end (v. 39) we find a definition of God
and of his works which is amplified in Pseudo-Jonathan.

**Ps J on Dt. 32, 39**
> ³⁹When the Word of YHWH shall appear in order to ran-
> som his people, it shall say to all the nations "Behold now that
> it is I who am, and who was, and who is to be*g* *and there is
> no other God outside of me, it is I who,* through my Word,
> *make man to live and make* him to die. I have smitten the people
> of the house of Israel, and it is I who will *heal* them at the end
> of days, and there is no person who delivers through my hand
> Gog and his armies whom I shall allow to engage in battle with
> them.

The praise of God is continued to the end of the song (v. 43)
with modest applications which do not modify the text's meaning. Thus we arrive at the prelude of the death of Moses.

*e*The text here contains a paraphrase of the word "fever."
*f*Edom is the cryptic designation for Rome.
*g*Compare the formula of Rev. 1, 8.

# 26

# THE DEATH OF MOSES
## Tg. of Deuteronomy 34, 1-15

The text of Pseudo-Jonathan is more developed than the other Targums:

> [1]And Moses climbed the plains of Moab *to the mountain of Nebo,* to the top of the heights opposite Jericho. And the Word of YHWH *made him behold all the mighty* of the land, the great feats that Jephthah of Gilead was to accomplish and the victories of Samson son of Maneah of the tribe of Dan; [2]and the thousand captains of the commanders of Nephtali who were to ally themselves with Barak and the kings who were to kill Joshua son of Nun of the tribe of *Ephraim,* and the great feats of Gideon son of Joash of the tribe of *Manasseh.* And all the kings of Israel, and the royalty of the house of Judah that governed in the country until the last Temple was devastated. [3]And the kings of the south who were to unite with the kings of the north in order to annihilate the country's inhabitants. And the Ammonites and the Moabites who were to vex Israel. And the exiles of the disciples of Elijah who were to be chased from the valley of Jericho and the exiles of the disciples of Elisha who were to be chased from the *city of the palm-trees* on account of their brethren of Israel, two hundred thousand men. And the anguish of each generation. And the punishment of Armilus[a] the impious and the ranks of Gog. But at the time of this great distress, Michael[b] will arise with mighty arm as liberator. [4]*And YHWH said to him:* Such is the end of the Word relative to the country, *and such is the country that I promised in solemn oath to Abraham, Isaac and Jacob* saying: "I will give it to your descendants. *Look upon it with your eyes, but you shall never cross unto it.*

[a]That is to say Romulus for Rome.
[b]Cf. Dan. 12, 1.

This annunciatory speech which considerably amplifies a simple text, is a pretext for evoking in advance numerous episodes of Israel's history up to the punishment of Rome alluded to in hints, and more or less confused with the traditional theme of Gog and Magog, those responsible for the final conflict. It remains to evoke the death of Moses himself:

> 'Moses, the leader of Israel, was born on the seventh of the month of Adar, and on the seventh of Adar he was withdrawn from the world. An echo from heaven said: "Come, all you who have come into this world, and see the afflictions of Moses who has so greatly toiled without being recompensed. But he has been magnified by four great crowns. The crown of the Law is his, for he has captured it from the heavens, and the glory of the Presence of YHWH appeared to him with two thousand myriads of angels and forty-two thousand chariots of fire. The crown of the priesthood belonged to him during the seven days of the investiture of the priests. The crown of royalty was conferred upon him by heaven but he did not unsheath a sword, nor tie a horse, nor lead an army. The crown of good renown, he acquired it through good works and his humility." *Thereupon Moses, servant of YHWH was withdrawn there,* in the country of Moab, *upon a kiss of* the Word of YHWH.

By recounting that God buried Moses, the Targum respects the haggadic development of Gen. 32, which shows the different examples given by God to human beings, by adding the burial of the dead. It ends with praise of Moses, a prophet the like of whom has never appeared again in Israel.

# II
# THE TARGUM
# OF THE PROPHETS

# 27

# ISAIAH'S VISION
## Tg. of Isaiah 6

The inaugural vision of Isaiah (Is. 6) is the subject of an amplification which does not modify its general tenor. Rather, it strongly develops its literalness either in order to add explanations or to exclude the anthropomorphisms. There is no special "actualization" of the text except at its end, which concerns the "remnant" of Israel. Elsewhere, we find mainly additions and equivalences.

> ¹*In the year that king Uzziah* was struck by leprosy, the prophet said: *I have seen* the glory of YHWH *seated on a high throne and lifted up* in the heavens above *and the Temple* was filled with the brightness of his glory. ²Sacred ministers stood *before* him. *Each one had six wings: with two he covered his face so as not to see, with two he covered his body, so as not to be seen,* with two he performed his ministry. ³And they received a response from one to the other and said: "*Holy* is, in the heavens above, the House of his Presence! *Holy* is, on the earth, the work of his might! *Holy,* for ever and ever the YHWH of Hosts! *The whole earth is suffused with the brightness of his glory!*"
>
> ⁴*And the supports of the threshhold* of the Temple *shook at the voice* of contemplation and the House of the Sanctuary was filled with darkness. ⁵*And I said: Woe is me, for* I have sinned. *For I am a man* liable to reproach, and I live *in the midst* of a *people sullied* by sins. For *my eyes have seen the glory* and the Presence of the *King* of the world without end, *YHWH of Hosts.*"

73

*⁶And one* of the ministers made his way *toward me,* and he had in His mouth a word that he had received from before his Presence on the throne of glory in the heavens *above the altar.* ⁷And he dispatched it *into my mouth saying: "Behold* I have put my words of prophecy in your mouth, and your *faults* shall disappear and your sins shall be *expiated."*

*⁸And I heard the voice* of the word of YHWH *that* said: *"Whom shall I send and who will go* to teach?" *And I said: "Here I am, send me."* ⁹And he said: *"Go,* and *you shall say to this people* that they *hear well but without understanding,* that they *see well,* but without *knowledge.*

¹⁰*Befoul the heart of this people, and make heavy their ears,* and close *their eyes,* lest they see with their eyes, and hear with their *ears,* and understand with their *heart,* and be *converted* and be forgiven.

¹¹*"And I said;* "Until when, YHWH?" And he said: *"Until the cities* are devastated, without inhabitants, and the houses, without men, and the land is ruined and devastated, ¹²and until YHWH has *removed the sons of men therefrom and* devastation waxes in the midst of the land. ¹³And if a tenth of them remain, they shall yet again be delivered to conflagration, *like the oak and the terebinth* that in the fall of their leaves resemble deadwood and until then, they are moist, so that there subsists in *them a seed.* Thus the exiled of Israel shall be reassembled and they shall return to their land, *for their stock is a holy seed."*

We can see that the original meaning of the primitive text is respected. But there is a glossed explanation that is incorporated into the text literally. In this respect the Targum smacks of a *midrash,* but it is a question of a superficial *midrash.* The actualization consists in transferring to the present time the ordeal announced by the prophet. From the historical calamities of Israel, the thought proceeds to the actual ordeal of Judaism, the desolation of Jerusalem and the great exile of all her offspring. But there remains a hope that turns hearts towards the future and the final ingathering of the dispersed. The prophet's fundamental message is thus extended to refer to the present time.

# 28

# PARAPHRASE OF THE SONG OF THE VINEYARD
## Tg. of Isaiah 5, 1-7

The Song of the Vineyard is allegorical. It unfolds in four tableaux: (1) the subject of the bad vineyard; (2) the invitation to judge addressed to the listeners; (3) the judgment of the great Judge; (4) the conclusion that applies the allegory. The targumist goes straight to the conclusion in order to develop, from one end of the text to the other, the history of Israel the transgressor. Here the words that come from the original text will be left in italics. All the rest is recomposed:

> ¹The prophet said: *I will sing* now *for* Israel, who is compared to a vineyard, race of Abraham, *my friend,*[a] *the song of my friend for his vineyard. My* beloved people, Israel, I had given them a heritage on a high mountain, *on a fertile* land. ²And I sanctified them, and I glorified them, and I established them like the seedling of a select vineyard. *And I built my* sanctuary *among* them, and *I* gave them *even* my altar so that they might atone for their sins. And I said that they *should perform* good works before me. And they, they have wrought works of wickedness.
>
> ³O prophet! Tell them: Behold the house of Israel has rebelled against the Law, and they have not wished to repent, *and now,* inhabitants *of Jerusalem and men of Judah,* pronounce *now a judgment* before *me* against *my vineyard!* ⁴What good did I say that *I would still do for* my people, *that I have not done for them? Why* did I say that they *should perform* good works before me? And why have they wrought *works* of *wickedness?*
>
> ⁵And *now* I will inform you of what I am going *to do for my people:* I will remove my Presence from them and *they shall be handed over* to pillagers. I will sack their sanctuaries and they shall be *handed over* to those who will *trample* upon them.

[a]Cf. Is. 41, 8.

> ⁶*I will make* fugitives of them; they shall be neither aided nor
> sustained, and they shall be dispersed and forsaken, and I will
> order the prophets not to prophesy prophecy *on them.*
> ⁷*Now,* the people of YHWH *of Hosts is the house of Israel,
> and the men of Judah are the plantation of his joy.* He had
> said that they should do *right, and lo* they are oppressors: that
> they should do *justice, and lo* they multiply sins.

After v. 1 the image of the vineyard disappears, and immediately follows: a strict historicization of the poem, the installation
in the holy land, the national glory, and the Temple and its lit-
urgy centered on the Day of Atonement. In response, Israel is
unfaithful to the Law. The text is actualized so as to provoke peni-
tence among the listeners. Stanza 2 reverts to the theme by elimi-
nating the poetry of the text. Stanza 3 ascribes to the prophet the
announcement of a punishment which no longer has the poetic
coloring of the original, but in which the situation of the dispersed
Jews at the time the targumist is explaining the text is recognizable. But who would have been able to imagine that the rain coming from the clouds represents the word of the prophet? Stanza
4 concludes logically by completing the actualization of the text.
It is a perfect example of rabbinic preaching on a prophetic text
where the content and setting of the text is transferred to the
present.

# 29

# SENNACHERIB BEFORE JERUSALEM
## Tg. of Isaiah 10, 32

Chapter 10 of Isaiah contains an evocation of a foreign invasion
which is restricted almost to an itinerary (Is. 10, 28-34). Step by
step we follow the progress of the army that invades the country
and marches on Jerusalem (vv. 28-31). This itinerary in no way
coincides with that of Sennacherib's invasion in 701, but the Targum of Isaiah has projected Sennacherib's invasion onto the text,

and adds a lengthy development to v. 32: "On this very day, at Nob, he shall shake his fist at the mountain of the daughter of Zion, the hill of Jerusalem." This development, abridged in a brief recension of the Tg. of Jonathan, unfolds at greater length in the rabbinic Bible of Venice. It is lengthier still in the two manuscripts (one of which is Vatican *Urbaniti* I) and, especially, in the marginal text of Codex *Reuchlin,* in which it is termed "Targum *Yerushalmi.*" This is the text reproduced here; by completing its recensions one with the other.[1]

> "When the day was still at its height and he had plentiful time to make entry, lo Sennacherib, the king of Assyria, struck camp and set up three bivouacs. Now he had brought with him four thousand golden seats upon which were seated sons of kings bedecked with the royal crown. And he had brought with him sixty thousand swordsmen and lancers, two thousand archers and men as swift as eagles who ran in front of him to the number of one hundred thousand. The shortage in his armies was of two hundred sixty-thousand less one - for it was to come to pass that his hosts were deficient on account of Gabriel, one of the Princes who officiate before YHWH.[a] The front of his cavalry, from end to end, measured forty parasangs.[b] [Thus had they come against Abraham, our father, when they hurled him into the fiery furnace. Thus are they to come with Gog and Magog, when the world shall have consummated its appointed time so that the Deliverance comes to pass.[c]
>
> They were divided into four armies, the first army, upon crossing the Jordan drank all the water of the Jordan. The second army, upon crossing the Jordan, drew water from the treads left by the hooves of the horses, and they drank the water. The third army, upon crossing the Jordan, did not find any water and it dug wells and drank the water.[d]
>
> The fourth army, upon crossing the Jordan, had in its ranks Sennacherib as well as Nebuchadnezzar, his son-in law Adra-

---

[1] *Revue Biblique,* 1983, 202–28.
[a] No explanation is given for this shortage.
[b] The parasang is the Persian mile, already known by Herodotus.
[c] Addition on the margin of the Codex *Reuchlin.*
[d] Cf. Is. 37, 25, probable source of the development relative to the six army corps.

melech, Sharezer and Esarhadron, his sons: they crossed the Jordan and the earth made the dust to rise from the dry soil.

He came and stationed himself *at Nob,* the city of priests, before the wall that is in Jerusalem. He began to speak and said to his troops: "Is that not there the city of Jerusalem against which I have mobilized all my armies, and against which I have gathered all my provinces? Lo, it is smaller and weaker than all the cities of the nations that I have vanquished by the strength of my hands." He rose against it and, moving his head from side to side, *he shook his fist at the mountain* of the House of the Sanctuary *which is in Zion* and at the courts that are *Jerusalem.*

It is at the end of the development that a connection is made with the biblical text. The purpose of all that precedes is to put this end in its proper place by assuring it of a context. Free rein is given to the imagination so as to construct the legend of Sennacherib and to describe his armies. Yet we come upon several biblical reminiscences. In the last of the army corps, the targumist accumulates all the biblical proper names that he can find, including that of Nebuchadnezzar who becomes Sennacherib's son-in-law! The figures given are obviously exorbitant. The text still fluctuates between thousands and myriads. It is possible to note in passing the addition of a recension that recalls Abraham's ordeal and foresees the "final conflict" between Gog and Magog. But it is the end of the text which is essential: it shows the defiance hurled by Sennacherib at the living God. We understand that this demands a reflection on the end of this impious king, as found in the Targum of the book of Kings.

# 30
# DEFEAT AND DEATH OF SENNACHERIB
## Tg. of Is. 10, 33-34 and of 2 Kings 19, 35-37

The end of Is. 10 contains a brief oracle which is independent of the evocation of the invasion:

> ³³Behold the Lord YHWH of hosts, shall lop off the boughs with violence: and the topmost heights shall be hewn and the haughtiest shall be humbled. ³⁴The forest thickets shall fall beneath the ax, and Lebanon shall fall beneath the blows of the Mighty One.

The Targum transforms this text into an announcement of Sennacherib's defeat and death.

> ³³Because Sennacherib, the king of Assyria, puffed himself up with pride, behold the Master of the world, YHWH *of* Hosts shall launch in the midst of his armies a massacre, like grapes being treaded in the wine-press, and the *tallest of them* in stature shall be shattered *and* the powerful *shall be humbled.* ³⁴And he will slaughter the strong men of his armies who played at being strong by the sword, and those who waged war, their corpses shall be flung upon the land of Israel.

This brief text is linked with the end of the siege of Jerusalem, such as it is described in Is. 37 and chiefly in 2 Kg. 19, 35-37, in which the Targum includes an addition from *Yerushalmi* in the margin of the Codex *Reuchlin*:

### Tg. of the 2 Kg. 19, 35-37
> ³⁵*And it came to pass on that night* — the night of the Passover — that the Word of YHWH spread panic in the armies of Sennacherib, king of Assyria, *and Michael,* the angel of YHWH, went forth and slew *185 thousand in the army of the Assyrians.* He shattered them with a blast of scorching breath, but the bodies subsisted. And *Sennacherib* his three sons and Nebuchadnezzaer, his son-in-law, arose at dawn, and they

looked and, lo, all were *dead* bodies, their breaths charred like cinders.

[36]"When they saw it was thus, all five *fled*. When they reached the proximity of Kardu,[a] Sennacherib found shavings of the wood of the Ark,[b] which glowed. He said: "Ah! It is the god who saved Noah from the Flood, as well as the creatures that were with him. Now, all the idols whom I have served would not have been able to save him. From this day forward, I will serve him: perhaps I shall be saved." He took them, and built the house of the idol *in the city of Nineveh* and he called it Nisroch. [37]*Now, while he was worshipping before Nisroch,[c] his idol, Amdrammelech and Sharezer, his two sons,* saw him. They said to each other: "Woe unto this old man who, during all his days, has served the idol! He has vexed and vanquished provinces. He has assembled armies in order to rise against Jerusalem by rebelling against the God of the heavens and of the earth, and he has seen the sign that the latter made for his people. For he has dispatched one of his servants, and the latter smote all the multitudes that were in them without weapons of war. And we, we have been saved. This is why it seemed fitting and proper to us to slay this haughty, this hardened one, because he has beheld the strength of the God of the heavens, when the latter did not make us perish." They went forth and they *slew him with the sword, then they fled to the land of* Kardu, a place where there was the group of exiles whom their father had banished. Immediately they proclaimed their freedom to them and they returned them to Jerusalem. And they left with them and they became proselytes. And it is they, Shemaiah and Avtalyon, the leaders of the Assembly.

It is not enough to amplify the account of the liberation of Jerusalem, already "haggadic" in the literalness of the book of Kings. It is necessary to explain two details on which the latter gives no information: the origin of the idol called Nisroch, and the motive that prompts the two sons of Sennacherib to kill him. On the first point, we find a trace of the legend which speaks of the part played by the wood of Noah's Ark. (This legend is still

[a]Kurdistan.

[b]Noah's ark.

[c]This name remains of unknown origin. The Targum offers no explanation.

alive today!) The king of Assyria is said to have fashioned his idol with this wood. Regarding the second point, the crime of the two sons is glorified as a just punishment for Sennacherib's hardening of heart. For the same reason the two sons of the king of Assyria are said to have converted to Judaism and eventually to have become the progenitors of the "pair" of scholars mentioned in the "chapters of the Fathers": Shemaiah and Avtalyon. The exact origin of these legends inserted in the thread of the narrative is unknown. But they tellingly show the role of the imagination in the construction of the targumic haggada. We also find some details which find a parallel in the Babylon Talmud. The mode of execution by which Sennacherib's armies were executed was already known in the *Apocalypse of Baruch* (toward the end of the first century), which attributes it to Gabriel and not to Michael.

# 31

# CONCERNING THE CAPSTONE TO THE FUTURE KING
## Tg. of Isaiah 28, 16-19

In the Hebrew text the brief oracle of Is. 28, 16-17a interrupts the poem which included vv. 14–15 and 17b–19. In the Targum the entire text is linked. The oracle becomes a response of God to the reasoning of the evil counsellors (28, 14-15), and there is no interruption between vv. 17a and 17b. Nevertheless, the ms. *Urbinati I* begins a new line before v. 16, so as to clearly highlight this oracle whose content is completely changed. Here we shall cite first v. 16 in the Hebrew in order to better show the difference.

> [16]This is why the Lord YHWH speaks thus: *Behold that I am preparing in Zion a stone, a stone of selection, a priceless block, laid down as foundation: "The one who shall believe shall not stumble."*

> [16]*This is why, thus speaks* YHWH-God:[a] Behold that I am
> preparing in *Zion* a King, a mighty King, strong and formidable.
> I will make him powerful and energetic, said the prophet. And
> the just who have believed in these things, when anguish shall
> arrive, they shall not be frightened. [17]*And I will set the Judg-
> ment,* established, *as a plumb-line of construction,* and Justice,
> as a leveling *stone. And my wrath shall set afire* your refuge
> of falsehood, and *because you have hidden from anguish, the
> nations shall exile you.*

Thus referring the text to the stone becomes a messianic oracle
in a very political sense. But it must not be forgotten that the New
Testament also reinterpreted this oracle by making Christ Jesus
the cornerstone upon which the spiritual edifice of the Church
rests (1 Pet. 2, 6-8). It is probable that the messianic interpretation attested by the Targum preceded its Christological application. Here the end of v. 17 is strictly linked to its beginning and
is the subject of a concrete explanation that addresses the condition of the dispersed Jewish people.

[a]Wherever the text cites "the Lord YHWH" the Targum manuscript translates
"YHWH—Elohim" because YHWH was rendered by "Lord."

# 32

# CONCERNING THE SCENE
# ON MOUNT MORIAH
## Tg. of Isaiah 33, 7-9

The text of the Targum of Isaiah is taken here from the Codex
*Reuchlin.* It concerns a marginal gloss that accompanies v. 7. The
gloss was probably the beginning of a prophetic reading of the
text which projects into it the scene on Mount Moriah as narrated
in Gen. 22.

[7]Behold when I revealed myself to Abraham and told him that I would give him Isaac, he believed my word. And after that, for the second time when I told him to offer him as holocaust, he did not hesitate: he went forth, he built the altar on Mount Moriah and offered him as holocaust. All the angels of up above, messengers of tremblings, messengers of fear, stood there and *cried out to the outside* of their posts: "Master of the world! Is not that Abraham the just there with a view to whom the world was established? You gave him a son at the end of one hundred years and you said to him: "It is through Isaac that descendants shall be named after you. . . ." Even the angels of peace, who dwell in the abode of the Presence, *wept with bitterness,* so much so that my mercy prevailed and I spared him. [8]Then the just who walk in the paths of the patriarchs *were desolate;* the pious who walk in the right paths before me, desisted: *they exchanged the precepts* of the Law. Because of that, *they withdrew from their cities* and went into exile. *The sons of men* were no longer *considered* before him. [9]Those who inhabited the *earth* went into mourning on account of *the ruin* and the sanctuary was desolate like the desert. The city of Jerusalem was desolate like the desert. And the high defensive walls, which were solid, were toppled over and demolished, *in Bethany and on Carmel.*

It must be recognized that the Hebrew text is very obscure and that it is difficult to give it a meaning which may serve as an immediate edification. The strategy employed, which consists in explaining through the text the Law, which has been linked to it, is skillful in its way but artificial. What is essential to retain is the composition of a scene in which one sees the angels commiserate at the moment when Abraham makes ready to perform his sacrifice. All of nature participates in this mourning and the desolation of Jerusalem is introduced in this context through another artifice. In fact, the content of each verse may be explained in terms of the general ideas that the targumist already had in mind.

## 33

# THE MESSIAH, SERVANT OF YHWH
## Tg. of Isaiah 42, 1-7

Christian theology has adopted the practice of setting aside the four "Servant Poems" in order to apply them to Jesus Christ. In the Targum we find another reading which is more or less directed against the Christian interpretation, but which continues the ancient Jewish interpretation which applied the texts to the community of Israel. Here they are read as compositions of Isaiah himself, in the setting of the broad context that constitutes the entire book particularly in chapters 40–45.

The first poem is applied to the Messiah, by reason of its wholly positive character. But the accent is placed on the work of the Messiah with a view to the restoration of Israel. It concerns Is. 42, 1-7:

> ¹*Behold my Servant* the Messiah, I will let him approach; my elect in whom my Word has delighted. I will put upon him my Spirit of holiness. He shall reveal my *Judgment to the nations.* ²He shall not cry out and shall not declaim and he shall not raise *his voice at large.* ³He shall not smite the humble who are like a *crumbled reed,* and he shall not extinguish the destitute who are like a *dwindling wick.* He shall present the Judgment in truth. *⁴He shall be neither weary nor fatigued, until he has established Judgment on earth and the isles await his law.*
>
> ⁵Thus speaks YHWH (. . .): *⁶I, YHWH, I have promoted you truly and seized you by the hand. And I will establish you and will set you as light of nations in order to open the eyes* of the house of Israel, they who are like the *blind* in relation to the Law. ⁷*In order to bring out* their exiled from among the nations, *they who are* akin to *prisoners,* and in order to deliver them from the bondage of the kingdoms in which they are detained like *prisoners of darkness.*

The retouchings permit an adaptation of the text to fit the classic representation of the Messiah in rabbinic theology: it is no longer a question of recognizing in the Servant Jesus the Messiah. At-

tention no longer focuses on the Law revealed to the nations but
on the *Judgment* (same word) that falls upon them, nor on the
light that is revealed to the nations to put an end to their blindness and enslavement, an enslavement which is one with the blindness and enslavement of Israel, but rather on the liberation of
Israel exiled and in bondage to the nations. Thus the primitive
plasticity of the text is completely transformed so as to adapt itself to the situation of Judaism in its ordeal.

# 34

# EXCERPT FROM THE SPEECH ADDRESSED TO THE SERVANT ISRAEL
## Tg. of Isaiah 49, 1-11

In Is. 49, 3 mention of the Servant *Israel* permits collective in-
terpretations of the entire text. We shall not examine here vv. 1–6
which are systematically amplified to correspond to this interpretation. Already in v. 6 the text shifts to the second-person plural
to prepare for the transformation of v. 7:

> [7]*Thus spoke YHWH the redeemer of Israel, its Holy One,*
> *to* those *who* are *despised among the nations, to* those who have
> been *slaves* among *the rulers: "Kings shall see* them *and there*
> *shall arise, princes, and they shall worship, on account of*
> YHWH, because *the Holy One of Israel is faithful and* he
> delighted *in thee.*

The shifting to the plural except in the last word—which is
illogical—presumes a collective application that was not in the
literal text: it is the meaning chosen in the whole of the passage.

# 35

# EXCERPT FROM THE "THIRD SONG OF THE SERVANT" Tg. of Isaiah 50, 4-11

This whole song is read as though speaking of the prophet himself. At the beginning of the text we find a complaint of the persecuted prophet (50, 4-9). But the end considerably develops a primitive sapiential text and describes the promised punishment to be inflicted upon the nations:

> [10]The prophet said: "The Holy One (Blessed be He) is about to say to all nations: *which among you is* the one among those that fear YHWH, that *listens to the voice of his servants* the prophets, that fulfills the Law in its tribulations like a man who *walks in the darkness and has no light? He hopes in the name of YHWH and has trust in the deliverance of his God."*
>
> [11]The nations respond and say before him: "O our Master! It is not possible for us to pore over the Law. For every day we are in conflict with each other in war. And when we have got the better of one over the other, [when] we have set their dwellings afire and deported their women, their children and their goods, our day is taken up by this matter and it is not possible for us to pore over the Law.
>
> The Holy One (Blessed be He!) responds and says to them: *"Behold, all of you, you poke the fire,* you brandish the sword. *Go,* fall *into the fire* that you have poked and by the sword that you have brandished! *This* has happened to *you* through the Word: *you* shall return to your desolation."

The additions have nothing to do with the texts that they amplify. They translate the general sentiment of oppressed Judaism towards the nations that persecute it by opposing their conduct to that of the faithful who "pore over the Law." The text could not be less universalist: it shows the nations as victims of the Law of talion, which is said to preside over their historical destiny.

# 36

# DISAPPEARANCE OF THE "SUFFERING SERVANT"
## Tg. of Is. 52, 13–53, 12

Isaiah's long poem (52, 13–53) poses a difficult problem to literal exegesis: whom is it about? An historical personage of the present or a figure of the future? An individual or a personified collectivity? Christian exegesis has applied the text to the suffering Jesus in order to read in it the sketch of the mystery of redemption. The Targum is a counter statement to this interpretation. Accordingly, it reclassifies all the expressions of the text so as to portion them out among the suffering Jews, the glorious Messiah and the nations doomed to disaster. It is a matter of a total recomposition in which the primitive literalness is resumed only for the purpose of turning it in a direction that corresponds to rabbinic theology. This way of operating is not ancient. In fact, since the Greek version of Isaiah, the text was applied to all the suffering Just in order to situate their suffering in relation to their final salvation and the salvation of their people.

> (52) *¹³Behold, my Servant* the *Messiah shall triumph; he shall be exalted, he shall grow, he shall become very powerful.* *¹⁴Just as* the house of Israel has hoped in him during the numerous days, for *their aspect was miserable* among the nations *and* their *appearance different from that* of the sons of men, *¹⁵*Thus shall he disperse *numerous nations, kings* shall keep silent in regard to him: they will place their hands over *their mouths; for they will have seen* what had *not been related to them and they will have seen what they had not heard being told.*
>
> (53) *¹Who would have believed this good tiding which is ours, and* the might of the strong *arm* of YHWH, *to whom has it been revealed?* *²*The just *shall increase before him like shoots* that bud, *and like a tree* that sends its roots into the water springs, so shall grow the holy generations on *earth* who had need of him. *His appearance* shall not be that of a man of the common run, nor his fear that of the ordinary man: his *bright-*

*ness* shall be the brightness of holiness, so that whoever *shall see* him shall contemplate him.

³Then the glory of all the kingdoms *shall be delivered to contempt* and will come to an end: they shall be infirm and suffering like a *man of sorrows* and *habituated* to illness; *and just as the face* of the divine Presence has withdrawn from us, they shall be held in *contempt and discredited.* ⁴*Then* he, he shall pray for our sins, and our iniquities shall be forgiven because of him. And we, we were *looked upon as impaired* by illness, *struck by God and humiliated.* ⁵*But he,* he shall build the sanctuary which has been defiled *by our sins,* delivered *because of our iniquities* and through his teaching his *peace* shall abound upon *us,* and because of our attachment to his words our sins shall be forgiven.

⁶*All of us, like sheep, we* have been scattered, we have been exiled, *each one following his own path,* and it was the good pleasure of YHWH *to forgive our sins to all* because of him. ⁷He prayed and his prayer has been granted. It was accepted before *he had opened his mouth.* He shall deliver the nations *like a lamb to the slaughter and like a sheep that keeps silent before its shearers,* and there shall be no person who *opens his mouth* before him nor who pronounces a word.

⁸He shall pull out our exiles from *chastisements* and punishment and the marvels that shall be worked for us during his days, *who* will be able to *relate them?* For he shall *remove from the land of Israel* the domination of the nations and he shall devolve upon them *the sins* of which *my people* has been guilty. ⁹He shall deliver *the impious* to Gehenna, and those who are *rich* in goods seized through force, to the death of perdition so that the *artisans* of *sin* do not endure and do not speak *deceit* with their *mouth.*

¹⁰*It was the good pleasure of* YHWH to refine and to purge the remnant of his people, so as to purify their *souls* of sins. *They shall see* the kingdom of their Messiah; they shall multiply *their* sons and *their* daughters and *shall prolong their* days, and those who fulfill the Law of YHWH *shall prosper,* according to his good pleasure. ¹¹He shall deliver their *soul* from the bondage of the nations. *They shall see* the punishment inflicted upon their enemies, *they shall sate themselves* on the spoils of their kings. Through his wisdom, *he shall justify* the just so as to submit many under the Law and *he* shall for their *sins.* ¹²*Then*

*I* will give him a *portion* of the spoils of the *numerous* nations,
and *he shall* share like a *booty* the goods of the *mighty* cities,
*in return for having delivered his soul to death* and subjected
the *rebels* to the Law. *And he,* he shall pray for the *numerous*
sins and the rebels shall be forgiven, thanks to him.

The transformation of the text so as to adapt it to the "classic" royal messianism is total. The only truly new point that is retained is the Messiah's prayer for the sinners of his people. Apart from that, all the difficulties are turned around even that of 53, 12 in which the Servant "delivers his soul to death." It is clear here that he does not die from it: it is an allusion to the struggles that he has sustained for his people. The image of the warrior Messiah is thus introduced in the most unexpected place.

# 37

# ISAIAH'S MARTYRDOM
## Tg. of Isaiah 66, 1

A Pseudo-epigraph that probably goes back to the first century of our era related the martyrdom of Isaiah the prophet, who was sawn in half at the orders of King Manasseh. The epistle to the Hebrews knows this legend and alludes to it (Heb. 11, 37). Two manucripts of the Targum of Isaiah furnish an additional text borrowed from the Targum *Yerushalmi* which reports the same event (marginal gloss of the Codex *Reuchlin* and an addition from the Vatican Codex *Urbinati 1*). The legend is coupled to the Targum of Isaiah 66, 1, which is a beginning of the liturgical reading. The text gives first of all the Tg. of Jonathan on this verse, then the haggadic development which states the prophecy in the frame of Isaiah's life and explains how his preaching entailed his martyrdom (cf. *Revue Biblique,* 1972, 511–43).

[1]Targum *Yerushalmi* of "the heavens are my throne." *Thus speaks* YHWH: The *heavens are the throne* of my glory *and*

the earth a footstool before me. And what is the place *of the house that you shall build* before me and *what is the place* of the house of *habitation* of my Presence?

Prophecy of Isaiah which he prophesied at the end of his prophetic mission in the days of Manasseh, son of Hezekiah, king of the tribe of the house of Judah, the fifteenth of Tammuz at the time when Mannaseh erected an idol in the Temple.[a] He prophesied to the people, the house of Israel: "*Thus speaks* YHWH: *the heavens are the throne* of my glory. And why do you puff yourselves up with pride before me on account of his House that was built by the hands of King Solomon. It is not true that the higher heavens and the lower heavens have not succeeded in containing the presence of my glory, according to that which is said through the medium of King Solomon: For who thinks and esteems that it truly pleased YHWH to have his Presence dwell in the midst of men who reside on the earth? Behold the heavens and the heavens of the heavens cannot contain the presence of my glory; much less this House that you have built.[b] In this hour, there is before me no pleasure in it, because you provoke wrath before me. And thus, behold that I am going to send for Nebuchadnezzar, and he shall destroy it, and he shall deport you from the city of Jerusalem."[c]

When Manasseh heard the words of Isaiah's warning, he was full of wrath against him. He said to his servants: "Run after him, seize him!" They ran after him to seize him. He fled from them, and a carob-tree opened its mouth and swallowed him. They brought saws of iron and they cut the tree, so that the blood of Isaiah flowed like water.

Is it not what is written: "And, moreover, Manasseh shed innocent blood in great abundance, until he filled Jerusalem from end to end; in addition to the sins that he committed and that he made Israel and those of the house of Judah commit, in order to do what is evil before YHWH."[d] That because he killed Isaiah who warned them and said: "Think not that it is for your sake that this House has been built. It is not even for the merits of your fathers, the just, that the Holy One—blessed

[a] See 2 Chr. 33, 7.

[b] Tg. of 1 Kg. 8, 27.

[c] Cf. 2 Kg. 23, 26 b.

[d] Tg. of 2 Kg. 21, 16.

be He!—made his Presence dwell in the midst of it. But at that hour, YHWH said: "*The heavens are the throne* of my glory and *the earth, a footstool* before me. *What is the house that you shall build* for my Name, and *what is the place* of the house of *habitation* of my Presence?"

The haggada forms a well-structured whole. Thanks to it we see how the legend of Isaiah's martyrdom could come into being: the text of 2 Kg. 21, 16 is referred to Isaiah. The punishment for the persecution of which Isaiah is victim is explained by the text, primitively anonymous, of 2 Kg. 23, 26f. Such is the frame in which the targumist sets the oracle of Is. 66, 1-2, supporting it on Solomon's prayer (I Kg. 8, 27). A single detail escapes any explanation: the folkloric touch of the carob-tree which opens in order to hide the prophet. This touch is universally preserved by the texts that relate Isaiah's martyrdom. Its aim is to explain that the blood of the prophet flows and fills Jerusalem. The lateral attestations of the story betray its antiquity. But it is only in the context of the Targum that we understand the literary origin. The latter, in the two attestations of it that remain, preserves an ancient tradition.

# 38
# PALESTINIAN TARGUM OF ISAIAH 66, 2

This time it is only the Vatican Codex *Urbinati 1* that preserves the Tg. *Yerushalmi* of Is. 66, 2, following the account of the prophet's martyrdom. The technique is the same: the quotation from the Hebrew text is followed by its Aramaic paraphrase after which comes an explanatory addition which is a veritable *midrash* on the verse:

> ²*And all these things, my strength has made them, and all those things did they* not *exist?* said YHWH. *And it is toward the one* who is before me that it is a delight *to look upon:* to-

ward the one who is *poor* and humble *of spirit and trembling* before *my word.* (Addition). On the one hand, as for signs and acts of power that have been performed for my people Israel, and that are to be performed for them, that is for the sake of the tribes. And on the other hand, the house of the sanctuary must be built for the sake of the tribes, according as is said in the holy Spirit through the medium of the Psalm of David. *"For there must the tribes go up*[a] *. . ."* and: *". . . the house of David* shall receive the royalty and it shall pronounce *a judgment* of truth for Israel."*[b] On the one hand, the world and all that which is in it was created only for their sake: the twelve months, and the twelve constellations that are in the firmament, the twelve hours that are in the day and the twelve hours that are in the night. And, on the other hand, the hosts of the heavens and of the earth have been created only for them, and it is "twelve tribes" that I have created. Did not all these things not exist? said YHWH. And it is *toward the one* that is before me that it is a delight to *look upon* "toward *the one who is poor* and humble *of spirit and trembling before my Word."*

The addition speculates on the number twelve by relating it to the twelve tribes which are not mentioned in this text of Isaiah. But it is the sanctuary, already mentioned, that is the leading theme, through the mediation of Ps. 122 where the Palestinian Targum is cited in a fragmentary form. The targumist introduces the principle that everything was created for Israel's sake and reflects the structure of the twelve tribes. It is, however, impossible to assign a date to this development, which is known from a later midrashic collection, the *Pesiqta Rabbati,* in the *Moussaf* for the feast of the Dedication of the Temple.

[a]Tg. of Ps. 122, 4.
[b]Tg. of Ps. 122, 5.

# 39
# AN ALLEGORY OF EZEKIEL
## Tg. of Ezekiel 16, 1-14

The text of Ezekiel 16 is a lengthy allegory that develops in a symbolic form the whole history of Israel: the girl foundling who is saved from death becomes an adult. She is adorned with jewels by her benefactor who marries her, but she is infatuated with her own beauty and gives herself up to prostitution. The targumist has perfectly understood this general meaning. But he suppresses all the poetry of the passage so as to substitute for it a rather dry summary of events, a summary he draws from the sacred books. Here we retain only the beginning of the fragment which suffices to show the genre of the operation.

> ¹*The word* of prophecy *was with me* before YHWH saying: ²*Son of man! Admonish* the inhabitants of *Jerusalem* and *make known* to them their *abominations.* ³*And you shall say: thus says YHWH-God* to the inhabitants of *Jerusalem:* your place of residence and your childhood are *of the land of the Canaanites.* There I revealed myself to your father Abraham among the apportioned animals, and I let him know that you would go down into Egypt, that with raised arm I would deliver you and that, through the merit of your fathers, I would drive away before you the *Amorites and Hittites.*[a] ⁴*And moreover,* when your fathers went down into Egypt, dwelling on a land that did not belong to them, they were enslaved and oppressed. The assembly of Israel resembled a new-born babe who is abandoned in the open field, whose *cord was not cut,* who had not been *dipped in water* to be washed, *who had not been salted with salt* and who *had not been wrapped in swaddling clothes.* ⁵The eye of the Pharaoh did not spare you in order to do you any good, to give you rest from your servitude, to *have pity* on you. He enacted against you a decree of extermination in order to have your males *thrown* into the River so as to make you perish at the time you were in Egypt. ⁶And in remembrance of the

[a]Hebrew: "your father was an Amorite and your mother a Hittite."

covenant of your fathers before me, I revealed myself in order to save you, for it was clear before me that you were oppressed by your bondage. And I said to you:[b] *"Through the blood* of circumcision, I will spare you, *through the blood* of the Passover I will deliver you."* *[7]I made you become myriads *like the plants of the field:* you have multiplied and reinforced yourselves and you have become families and tribes, and thanks to the proper works of your fathers, the time of deliverance of your assembly came to pass for you were enslaved and oppressed. [8]Then I revealed myself to Moses in the bush, for it was clear before me that *the time* of your deliverance had come. And I made a protection above you through my Word and I effaced your sins and promised through my Word to deliver you, just as I had promised it to your fathers, *said* YHWH-God, so that you might be a people that does service before *me.* [9]I will deliver you from the bondage of Egyptians and I will make cease the power of their worship upon you, and I will lead you away in freedom. [10]*And I will clothe you with embroidered garments* from the best of your enemies, and I put *shoes of fine leather* on your feet. And I sanctified among you the priests so that they might serve before me with *turbans* of fine linen and the high priest with *garments* of varicolored fabric. [11]And I established you through the establishment of the words of the Law, written on the two stone tablets and given to the hands of Moses, and I sanctified you through the holiness of my great name. [12]I placed among you the ark of my covenant, and the cloud of glory made shade above you, and an angel sent by me marched at *your head.* [13]I set my Tent among you, decked with gold and silver, with tapestries of fine linen and *varicolored fabrics* and *embroideries.* And I made you *eat* manna which was good like the cakes of fine *flour* and like *honeycomb.* You became enormously rich and strong, and you prospered and dominated over all the *kingdoms.* [14]The *renown* of the assembly of Israel went forth for you *among the nations, for your beauty, for it was perfect,* my glory *that I had placed upon you, said YHWH-God.*

This passage of the text suffices to show the procedure employed by the targumist. He explains the meaning of all the metaphors

---

[b]Hebrew: "live in your blood."

of which the allegory is woven. It is meditation on the past of
Israel that underlines God's goodness to his people. Accordingly,
the ingratitude of the people is underlined by all its sins, past and
present. The biblical text thus takes on the meaning which was
given to it in the synagogues. We have not tried to reproduce all
the details to show how they are transformed, on occasion in the
wrong sense. Wherever the Hebrew text bears the words: "the
Lord YHWH," in the Targum we read: "YHWH-God."

# 40
# THE RESURRECTION OF THE DEAD
## Tg. of Ezekiel 37, 1-14

The Targum of Jonathan on Ezek. 37, 1-14 follows the Hebrew
text rather closely. But A. Diez Macho has published a fragment
of the Tg. *Yerushalmi* that notably develops this text. It is not
certain that Tg. *Yerushalmi* covered the whole book of Ezekiel.
This passage was probably a liturgical reading tied to a text of
the Pentateuch, probably Ex. 13, 17, if we are to believe the Tg.
of Pseudo-Jonathan which introduces a summary of it at this point
(see this text). The language of the fragment has been aligned with
that of the Tg. of Jonathan. In v. 7 an altogether adventitious
element has been introduced into the logical development of the
text. But the Tg. of Ex. 13, 17 gives an explanation of it (cf. p. 42):

> [1]The prophet Ezechiel said: when the Master of the World
> made me know the redemption that he would accomplish for
> the remnant of Israel which had been dispersed among the na-
> tions, I thought in my heart: "What will become of the dead
> who died in exile?" [Thereupon] rested *upon me* a spirit of
> prophecy [come] from before YHWH *and it set me down in
> the valley of* Doura and it was *full of human bones.* [2]*And the
> spirit made me pass all around above them.* They were the re-
> mains of thirty thousand foot-soldiers who went out of Egypt

thirty years before the appointed time, and the Philistines slew them. *And, lo, the bones were very numerous on the surface of the valley and they were very dry.* *³And the spirit said to me: "Son of Adam, will these bones live (again)?" And I said:* "It is a matter unveiled before you." *⁴And the spirit said to me: "Prophesy upon these bones and you shall say: 'Dry bones, receive the word* of prophecy of YHWH!'" *⁵Thus speaks* YHWH-God *to these bones. "Behold I make my Spirit enter into you, and you shall live. ⁶And I will put nerves upon you, and I will make flesh arise upon you, and I will spread skin upon you, and I will place spirit in you and you shall live. And you shall know that I am* YHWH." *⁷And I prophesied just as the spirit had prescribed to me. And it came to pass that at the voice of my prophecy, there was a trembling, and the bones came together, one to the other.* The vessels were in service in the house of God, and Nebuchadnezzar, king of Babylon, had carried them off. And at the very moment when the prophet was prophesying upon them, king Belshazzar was drinking from one.[a] The angels smote this impious one on the mouth and at that very same moment the bones came together with their neighbors. The king trembled exceedingly and his complexion changed, and his thoughts tormented him, and the joints of his loins slackened, and his knees knocked against each other.[b] *⁸And I saw, and lo, nerves and flesh arose on them, and the skin stretched over both and there was no spirit in them. ⁹And the spirit said to me: Prophesy to the Spirit, prophesy, son of Adam! And you shall say to the Spirit: Thus speaks YHWH-God: from the four winds, come, Spirit, and enter into these corpses, and they shall live! ¹⁰And I prophesied just as the spirit had prescribed to me. And the Spirit entered into them and they lived (again) and they arose to their feet, a very, very numerous host.* They all arose, except for a man who did not arise. The prophet began to speak and said before YHWH: "What are the works of this man, why have all those lived (again) and he has not lived (again)?" The angel of YHWH replied and said to the prophet: "He practiced lending against security and usury and this is why he did not merit to live (again) in the midst of his brethren." *¹¹And he said to me: Son of Adam,* through what

---

[a] The Tg. of of Ex. 13, 17 explains that the vessels had been made of bones.
[b] Quotation from Dn. 5, 6.

I have done *to these bones* you will know what I (will do) for the sons of Israel who shall die in exile. For the descendants of Israel say: "When we shall die, we shall not see the redemption that YHWH is to bring about for Israel. *Our bones* shall be *dry* and *our hope shall be no more and our trust shall perish.* " [12]This is why you prophesy thus, and *you shall say: "Thus speaks YHWH-God,* Behold that I gather your dispersed and *I will open the graves of your dead, and I will let your* [buried] *arise and I* [*will lead you*] *to the land of Israel.* [13]*And you shall know that I am YHWH when I will open the graves of your dead and when I will make your dead* rise (again), *O my people! And I will place my spirit in your dead and they shall live and I will let them dwell on your land, and you shall know that I am YHWH. I have decided through my Word and I will fulfill it, said YHWH.* "

The addition of v. 2, which introduces a concrete element into the symbolic scene of Ezek. 37, reverts to the legendary theme that the Tg. of Pseudo-Jonathan preserved in the context of Ex. 13, 17 and which we also find in the Tg. of the Chronicles on I Chr. 7, 21. It does not open up into a perspective of universal resurrection, but only into the idea of the universal participation of the exiled Jews in the final "redemption" (or deliverance). God can make the dead live again. But the conception of this "life" of all the ransomed and of all the exiled, finally gathered in the holy land, remains very material. The "world to come" will resemble the present world, except on one point: the suppression of sin. The addition of v. 10, poorly linked to the context, appears as a moralizing gloss to put readers or listeners on guard against usurious loans. But it is only a literary element. The text of Ex. 37 is interpreted not as a metaphorical resurrection of *the people* but as a return to life of the individuals who died before the day of the great "Deliverance."

# 41

# TARGUMIC ADDITION ON
# HOSEA'S VOCATION
## Tg. of Hosea 1, 2-3

The Targum tries to explain why God could give Hosea so scandalous an order: to wed a whore. It makes us understand the reason for this order by reference to the tenderness of God's heart.

¹*Beginning of the Word of YHWH through Hosea. YHWH said to Hosea:* "Go! Prophesy a prophecy for those who dwell in the guilty city and who continue to sin. *For* the inhabitants of the country are straying far from the service *of* YHWH."

Hosea replied and said before the Holy One (Blessed be He!): "If Israel sins before you, exchange them for another people!"

This is why the Holy One (Blessed be He!) said in regard to him that Hosea would have to learn from Moses, his servant, who had prayed for Israel and petitioned favor for them and said: "And now, will you not remit their faults? If not, expunge me from the books that you have written." It is not in accord with the one who does not ask for mercy before me, but who says: "Exchange them for another people."

"Now, therefore, I am going to order him to marry a whore and she will bear him children. Then I will ask him to exchange her and he shall know what agitation dwells in the heart of a man who exchanges his wife and his children." This is why the Holy One (Blessed be He!) *said to Hosea; "Go, wed a whore* and she shall bear you *children of whoredom!"*

*So he went forth and took Gomer, daughter of Diblaim.* "Gomer" because everybody paid and coupled with her,[a] "Diblaim" because she coveted men for herself like one covets a cake of figs.[b]

*And she conceived and she bore him* children, two sons and a daughter and God said to him: "Exchange this whore and her children, for she is a whore and her children are *the chil-*

---

[a]Pun on the root *Gar.*

[b]Pun on "cake of figs." *(d'bill'ta/Diblaim).*

dren *of whoredom!"* He replied and said before him: "For mercy's sake, Master of the World! Was it not by you that I was summoned to take her as a wife, and now that she has borne me two sons and a daughter you prescribe to me that I exchange her? May it please you to spare me and not to separate me from my children!" The Holy One (Blessed be He!) replied and said to him: "Prophet Hosea! Did you not have to learn from your own words? For you do not want to exchange a whore wife and the children of whoredom, how then did you tell me to exchange my beloved children, the children of Abraham, Isaac and Jacob, who have walked before me in truth and justice with a perfect heart?"

Hosea began to speak again and said before the Holy One (Blessed be He!): "I have sinned before you, YHWH." He replied and said to him: "I will not receive you, until you bless Israel and you prophesy good things for them!" So Hosea opened his mouth and said on the subject of Israel: *"The number of the children of Israel shall be as the sand of the sea"* (Hos. 3, 2).

This amplification of the text needs no commentary. God commands the prophet to wed a whore only so that God's mercy may be displayed. Hosea understands through his own experience why God is so attached to his sinful people.

# 42

# THE DAY OF THE CONSOLATION OF THE DEAD
## Tg. of Hosea 5, 15–6, 3

In some modern translations there is a break in the text between Hos. 5, 15 and 6, 1. But the synagogal reading is continuous. The Targum also directly links these fragments. The principal interest lies in the transformation of v. 6, 2. Literally it reads: "After two days, he shall make us live again; on the third day he will raise us, and we shall live in his presence." The text has been completely transformed.

> (5) ¹⁵I will remove my presence. *I will return to my holy abode* which is in the heavens, *so that they recognize that they have sinned,* so that they pray before me when that shall distress them, *so that they seek my fear.*
>
> (6) ¹They shall say: "*Come and let us turn to the* service of YHWH. For he *who has shattered us, he will heal us,* and he who has brought a catastrophe upon us, he will set us at rest. ²*He will make us live again* on the day of the consolations that are to come; on the day of the revivification of the dead *he will raise us up and we shall live before him.* ³*Let us learn, let us try to know* the fear of YHWH: *like the light of the morning* that shines upon his going forth, he will make blessings *fall upon us* like a heavy *rain* and *like a sudden autumn shower that moistens the earth."*

The dialogue continues as in the Hebrew text. At the beginning and at the end, the changes are slight. But v. 2 completely transforms the original by introducing the theme of the resurrection of the dead. It shows how the Jewish tradition has understood "the third day" of Hosea in a symbolic sense that has nothing of a chronological character. A list of passages in the sacred books where the "third day" is mentioned has been preserved in several places in the *Midrash Rabba:* it shows that it always concerns a day of salvation and of deliverance, and it ends with "the day of the consolation of the dead" according to Hos. 6, 2. This interpretation is the backdrop against which the third day as the day of the resurrection of Christ in the New Testament is said to be "according to the scriptures" (1 Cor. 15, 4). The reference is to the Scriptures interpreted by tradition as the Targum here attests.

# 43

# SONG OF HABAKKUK
## Tg. of Habakkuk 3

The song of Habakkuk is one of the most difficult passages of the Old Testament where it is most difficult to follow the development of the thought and to explain the variety of the images. This is one more reason why the Targum takes it up and links to it all that its phrases can suggest. Here we are not quoting the ordinary text of the rabbinic Bibles (reproduced in the London *Polyglot*), but that of the Codex *Reuchlin,* which is somewhat more ample, according to the editions of Merx (*Chrestomatha targumica,* pp. 104f.) and of Sperber (without vocalization). Each verse is commented on in isolation in a more or less developed paraphrase. None follow the literalness of the Hebrew, which at times is totally lost sight of.

> [1]Prayer through which prayed Habakkuk, the prophet, when a revelation was made to him on the matter of the respite that God has given to the impious. This prophet Habakkuk fashioned an image[a] and he stood in front of it, and began to speak thus: "His name is living and lasting! I will not go away from this image until someone makes me see the judgment that is to come." The Holy Spirit replied and spoke to him thus: "Prophet Habakkuk! As regards the respite that is given to the impious, if they convert to the Law with a perfect heart they shall be forgiven. All the sins of the house of Israel shall be before me as unawareness."
>
> [2]YHWH, *I have heard the tidings* of your might, what you have wrought for the generation of the Flood at the beginnings, *and I was afraid.* And so, as regards the punishment that you have caused to descend upon the men of Sodom because they had aroused a wrath before you: I have heard *and I have trembled.* YHWH how great are *your works* and your signs, powerful! For you give a respite to the impious in order to see if they return to the Law with a perfect heart, and they have not

[a]Lacking here is a precise description of the kind of image.

returned. And they, they arouse wrath before you, *in the midst of the years* of which you have said that the world would be renewed by the just, and in your wrath you have flared up against the impious: you shall recall your *mercy* toward the just and you will have love for them.

[3]Upon giving the Law to his people, *God* revealed himself from the heights and the *Holy One, from the mountain of Paran* in the power of the centuries. The heavens were covered with the brightness of his glory and all the earth was suffused with words of his praise.

[4]And *the splendor* of his glory revealed itself as the splendor of the day of the Beginnings, and sparks flashed from his chariot of glory. There he revealed his Presence which was hidden from the sons of men.

[5]*Before him* was sent the angel of *Death* and his Word burst forth like a flame of fire.

[6]He revealed himself and he caused the earth to tremble, and he caused the Flood to come upon the people of the generation that had transgressed his Word. And, also, a second time, when they sinned before him through their sins and he confounded the Nations.[b] And the *eternal mountains* were split, the temporal heights, he smote them: the strength of the word is his.

[7]When the house of Israel practiced the worship of idols, I delivered them into the hands of Cushan the sinner.[c] And when they converted in order to fulfill the Law, I made signs for them and wrought great feats: I delivered them from the hand of the *Midianites* through the hand of Gideon, son of Joash.

[8]Behold *against* the kings and their hosts, which were numerous like the waters of the *Flood,* there was a wrath before you YHWH. *Your wrath* was against the kings and in the sea you make them know the punishment of your might, for you revealed on the chariots of glory your Presence to your people, might and deliverance.

[10]When you revealed yourself on the mountain of Sinai, *they saw* your glory. The mountain shook. The clouds of rain dissolved. *The abyss raised its voice.* The hosts *above,* amazed, *stood up.*

[b]Allusion to the tower of Babel.

[c]Cf. Jg. 3, 3.

<sup>11</sup>Moreover, when you made signs for Joshua on the plain of Gibeon when against him arose and descended upon him the five kings—the king of Jerusalem, the king of Hebron, the king of Jarmuth, the king of Lachisch and the king of Eglon, *the sun and the moon stood still* in their places for twenty-six hours at your word.*[d]* They had risen in force, your voice obtained the victory.

<sup>14</sup>You divided the sea with the rod of Moses, and the heroes, chiefs of the armies of Pharaoh who had schemed plots against your people, you swept them away through the blast of the whirlwind and drowned them in the sea of Reeds because they had detested and subjugated your people and they had secretly held counsel to plan their destruction.

<sup>15</sup>You revealed yourself on the sea in your chariot of glory, *in the piling of abundant waters.*

<sup>16</sup>Babylon said: "*I have heard,* and the kings *trembled* before the judgment by which the Egyptians were judged. *At the sound* of these words, *my lips quivered,* trembling seized the sages. And in this place where we dwelt, I trembled because he had left me in anguish for a day: at the time when *I make go far* from me the deportation of my people, he will shatter me."

<sup>17</sup>For the kingdom of Babylon *shall not endure* and and will not let a tyrant rule over Israel, the kings of Media shall be exterminated, and the heroes of Greece shall not have the upper hand. The Romans shall be exterminated and shall not lay tribute upon Jerusalem.*[e]*

<sup>18</sup>This is why, for the sign and the deliverance that you will work for your Messiah and for the remnant of your people which shall endure, your name shall be praised, said the prophet. And I, in the name of YHWH, I will rejoice and *I will exult because of the God* who works *my deliverance.*

<sup>19</sup>God, YHWH, who helps me through *strength* and *makes my feet light as those of does,* and who *shall establish me* upon his mighty house, him through whom are *the victories* and the great feats, and before whom I will play *music in my hymn.*

---

*[d]* Summary of Jos. 10; Jos. 10, 13 speaks of a "delay" but the day begins in the evening.

*[e]* Classic theme of the four empires.

It is clear that the text is totally recomposed. As we have seen before, the penchant of the rabbinic tradition to explain the text by reference to the historical events of Israel's past: punishments of the Flood, of Sodom, of the Egyptians, of the kings allied against Joshua, of the Midianites—in the context of waiting for the final liberation to be accomplished by the hand of the Messiah. All this, more or less easily, links up with the literary fragments of the text. All the metaphors of the text are exploited, or better, historicized. The remembrance of Sinai dominates the perspective because it is the center of salvation history and controls its interpretation. One is very far from a literal translation. Moreover, the recension usually cited is not more literal, but it contains fewer developments on certain points. Verses 6-10 and 12-19 are identical in the two recensions. We have been able to note in passing the general method of the targumist: each verse is read in Hebrew in an independent way and immediately paraphrased, with no regard whatsoever for its context. This permits the targumist to introduce toward the end of the text the theory of the "four kingdoms" which concludes with the evocation of Rome and the announcement of its final fall.

# 44

# A MESSAGE OF HOPE
## Tg. of Zechariah 2, 14-15

The text of Zech. 2, 14-15 is almost identical to that of Wis. 3, 14-15. Hence the targumist refers to chapter 3 of Wisdom so as to amplify the message of hope contained in these two verses; he reproduces almost entirely vv. 5, 7-8, 10, 12-13 and 15 of an ancient paraphrase, which is lengthier than that of the existing Targum of Jonathan, but placed in a different order. At the end, he draws inspiration from Is. 66, 20. A single manuscript in the British Museum gives this lengthy text (BM Add 26879). By comparing it with that of the classic Tg., it can be noted that the latter is a reduction of it, intended to effect a connection with the Hebrew text by way of slight additions. We have here in capital letters, the text that corresponds to the Hebrew. Concerning the text of the Tg., cf. *Revue Biblique,* 1966, 197–211.

### Hebrew text of Zech. 2, 14-15

[14]"SHOUT AND REJOICE, DAUGHTER OF ZION, FOR BEHOLD I AM COME TO DWELL IN YOUR MIDST— ORACLE OF YHWH. [15]NUMEROUS NATIONS SHALL ATTACH THEMSELVES TO YHWH ON THAT DAY: THEY SHALL BECOME FOR YOU A PEOPLE AND THEY SHALL DWELL IN YOUR MIDST, AND YOU SHALL KNOW THAT YHWH OF HOSTS HAS SENT ME TO YOU.

[14]SHOUT and give praise, gathering OF ZION BECAUSE the glory of YHWH is revealing itself and the world shall glow with the brightness of his glory. For he has promised ( = said) to make DWELL his *Presence* IN YOUR MIDST ( = Zech. 3, 15 a, 15b) for it is excluded before him that he fabricate a lie (Tg. Wis. 3, 5) and he does not repent of what he has promised. *Behold, like the splendor of morning that comes and seizes* the whole world more than all, in *a like manner* his praise, and his glory, and judgment [come forth] (Tg. Wis. 3, 5). Behold that you, House of Israel, when you hear the teaching of the Law, *you shall have naught to fear from the evil* that comes into the world ( = Tg. Wis. 3, 15c), *because I will leave in your midst a humble people [. . .] in the mouth of whom no lying tongue shall be found* ( = Tg. Wis. 3, 12-13); men for the sake of whom the great people *shall be nourished and shall continue, and there shall be no person who shakes his head* at the name of YHWH. [15]And you [members] of the House of Israel, people of YHWH, apply your heart, from this day and henceforth, to my fear *and convert yourselves from your wicked ways and from your corrupted works* (Tg. Zech. 1, 4). But I have said to the House of Israel: "If you consider my Word, *if you fear me, and hearken to the teaching of* my Law, *I will not tear out your feet from the land of the house of Presence, and all the benefactions that I had promised to your fathers, I will have them come about for you* for the sake of your fathers, the just (Tg. Wis. 37a). And the descendants of Israel were not able to apply their soul to the words of the prophets (cf. Tg. Zech. 1, 4b) but, on

the contrary, *they have hastened to make worse their works* (Tg. Wis. 3, 7b) and they have not turned away from their wicked works and corrupted ways, [. . .] *and on the day in which I will reveal myself in order to judge* the world, I will judge them *because* the decision has been taken in my presence *to assemble the nations,* the fatherlands and the tongues *and to have kingdoms appear so as to pour upon them my fury and the might of my wrath* [because in the fire of my punishment . . .] until *all the impious of the earth disappear* from before me ( = Tg. Wis. 3, 8). And if the descendants of Israel turn away from their ways I will not pour out my fury upon them and I will have pity on them for the love of their fathers, the just, and I will gather their *deportations* from the nations *to which they have been deported* (cf. Tg. Wis. 3, 10), *and all the nations,* the fatherlands, *the tongues* and the kingdoms (c. Is. 66, 18a) are to carry them upon their shoulders and bring them like offerings (cf. Tg. Wis. 3, 10b and Is. 66, 20a) *and they shall become before me a beloved* people *and I will make my Presence* DWELL IN THEIR MIDST, AND YOU SHALL KNOW THAT YHWH OF HOSTS HAS SENT ME TO PROPHESY FOR YOU.

The existing text of the Targum of Jonathan has only preserved traces of this lengthy development for the purpose of linking it up with the Hebrew text. On the basis of it we can almost reconstruct the ancient Targum of Wis. 3, 5-15, the fragments of which are integrated here in a different order. The themes introduced into this development are: the invitation to conversion; the exhortation to the practice of the Law; the threat of the Judgment; the remembrance of the promises attached to fidelity; and the final perspective of hope. But recourse to Is. 66, 18-20 permits the elimination of the universalist perspective introduced by the reference to Zech. 2, 5 and the reversion to a strict religious nationalism. There is in it an echo of the rabbinic theology which followed the two catastrophes of the years 70 and 135, when Judaism withdrew within itself in order to assure its survival.

# 45
# THE MESSAGE OF EPHRAIM
## Tg. of Zechariah 12, 9–13, 1

The obscurity of Zechariah in its second part (9-4) is proverbial. We find mention of the mysterious "pierced" person (12, 10) whom critics fail to identify. The Greek translation of the passage by Theodotion is taken up in the Gospel of John and applied to Christ on the cross (Jn. 19, 37). The primitive targumist (Tg. *Yerushalmi*) profited from it in order to introduce at v. 10 an enigmatic "Messiah son of Ephraim" who plays a role in the final battle against Gog. His text is not followed in the Tg. of Jonathan that draws closer to the Hebrew text. We shall connect the beginning of chapter 13, which the Tg. of Jonathan likewise amplifies, with this passage.

> (12) *⁹And it shall come to pass at that time that I will try to annihilate all the nations* that gather together *and come against Jerusalem.* ¹⁰And I will *set upon the house of David and upon the inhabitants of Jerusalem the spirit* of prophecy and of true prayer. After which the Messiah son of Ephraim shall set forth to lead the struggle with Gog, and Gog shall kill him before the gate of Jerusalem and they shall ask me: "Why have the nations *pierced* the Messiah son of Ephraim?" *And they shall grieve over him like the father and the mother grieve over an only child and they shall mourn for him like* they *mourn for their first-born.* ¹¹*At that time the mourning in Jerusalem shall grow,* like the mourning of Ahab son of Omri who slew *Hadad-Rimmon* son of Amon who was slain by Pharaoh the Cripple in the valley of *Megiddo.*

Thus is the "pierced one" identified here. But the tradition of the Messiah son of Ephraim is not very ancient; at most it goes back to the adventure of Par-Kosiba, killed in August 135. Hypothetically, this Messiah is introduced in a tableau of "the End" in which Gog intervenes. The lamentation and the mourning is thus explained. In v. 11 the Tg. explains two enigmatic allusions by referring to 1 Kg. 15, 18 and 20, 34–37 (by way of a confused chronology) and then to the death of Josiah (by way of a pun on the name of the Pharaoh Neco). The end of the chapter more or less follows the Hebrew text. But we find its amplification in the beginning of the following chapter:

> (13) [1]*At that time,* the teaching of the Law, *shall be revealed* as a *fountain-head for the house of David* and for *the inhabitants of Jerusalem* and I will remit their *faults,* as one is purified by the water of the aspersion and by the ashes of the cow of the offering for sin.

The Law is introduced through allegory and the purification of sins is made specific by two allusions to the rites prescribed by the Law, although the rite of the reddish cow had become impossible since the destruction of the Temple. But the Targum speaks of it as though it were still being practiced.

# III
# TARGUM
# OF THE PSALMS
# AND
# OF THE FIVE SCROLLS

# 46

# TARGUM OF PSALM 45

In a literal sense Ps. 45 is a nuptial song, but Jewish tradition has tended to allegorize it as it did for the Song of Songs. It is this allegorization that the Targum assembles: the king and his spouse are the Messiah and the Assembly of Israel. Here we shall leave aside vv. 1-2 which are only an introduction to the theme.

³Your *beauty,* O king Messiah, is better than *that of the children* of men; the spirit of prophecy has *been placed upon* your lips; *this is why God has blessed you forever and ever.* ⁴*Gird your sword on your thigh like a valiant warrior* so as to slay kings with princes; it is your *honor* and your *prestige,* and your prestige is great. Thus you shall succeed in *riding* upon the royal horses, ⁵*with a view to faith, to truth,* to humility and *to justice,* and YHWH will teach you how to work wonders with *your right hand. . . .*

⁷*The throne* of your glory, YHWH has established it *for ever and ever. Your royal sceptre is a sceptre of rectitude.* ⁸And you, O king Messiah, because *you have loved justice and hated impiety,* YHWH, *your God has anointed you with the oil of joy in preference to your fellows. . . .*

¹⁰The provinces of the kingdoms come to visit your countenance at the appointed time. The book of the Law is *at your right side,* written on your splendid copy as though on *fine gold* coming from *Ophir. . . .*

¹¹*Listen,* assembly of Israel, to the Law from his mouth, and you shall see the marvels of his works. You *shall incline your ear* toward the words of the Law. You *shall forget* the evil works of the impious of *your people* and the house of idols that you

have served among *your fathers.* [12]*And thus the king shall de-sire your beauty, for it is he who is your master and you shall adore him.* [13]And the inhabitants of the city of *Tyre* shall come to present themselves, *the richest of the nations* shall hasten toward the sanctuary. [14]All the best, the most beautiful, the most desirable of the riches of the provinces, and the treasures of kings that are hidden inland, they shall offer them as oblations before the King and as gifts to the priests in multi-colored vest-ments of glittering gold. [15]*In embroidered vestments,* they shall take these vestments before the king of the world and the rem-nant of their fellows who are dispersed among the nations shall be led *in joy* before you in Jerusalem. [16]They shall be *with joy* and gladness and *they shall enter* the Temple of the King of the world. . . .

These excerpts show the genre of the haggadic development. The latter combines themes of rabbinic theology. The praise of the Messiah to come presents his liberating and just kingship. The assembly of Israel is characterized by its attachment to the divine Law. The procession of the nations that come to Jerusalem broadens the tableau. But all remains centered upon the people of God. The oblations of the nations arrive at the Temple where the cult and the priesthood are said to be restored. In this con-text the homages paid to the King must be understood in terms of God and not in terms of the king Messiah: God is the "king of the world." The literal text of the Psalm is adapted to express all these themes. One should not think of a very ancient commen-tary here. Nevertheless, the messianic interpretation would not be understood from the text if it were not traditional. Rabbinic theology has always reacted against the Christian usage of the texts. Yet, Ps 45 is the subject of christological interpretation in the New Testament (Heb. 1, 8-9).

# 47

# TARGUM OF PSALM 68

The text of the rabbinic Venice Bible, resumed in the London *Polyglot,* is compared with ms. no. 5 of the Library of the University of Madrid, prepared by Alfonso de Zamora for the Alcala *Polyglot,* whose recension is followed by the Antwerp *Polyglot.* Inspiration is drawn from the two texts which do not always coincide but which complete each other so as to give a "mixed" translation, which renders the text more intelligible in the difficult passages. The Targum is, in reality, a *midrash* of the Hebraic Psalm whose text is particularly difficult to explain in the literal sense. The haggada thus proposed offers intelligible meanings, with, at times, two explanations of the more obscure passages.

¹To praise. Through the *hands of David.* Praise and song.
²*Let God arise, and his enemies will scatter, and his haters shall flee before him.* ³*As smoke is dispersed, they shall he dispersed, and as water melts before fire, so shall perish the impious before God.* ⁴*And the just shall rejoice* and exult *before God and they shall he gladdened* in joy.

⁵*Praise before God!* Praise *his* glorious *name!* Exalt the one who is seated upon his glorious throne in the *clouds!* The one whose name is Yah, *and exult* before him! ⁶The Father of orphans, the Judge of widows, is *God in* the residence of *the house of his holy Presence.* ⁷It is God *who* joins together the *solitary* unwedded parties[a] in order to build with them *the home.* It is he who contrived to bring out the children of Israel who were *prisoners* in Egypt: because of the works of their fathers who were noble, he delivered them with great pomp. But Pharaoh and his army who had refused to let them go out *encamped in barren places.*

⁸*O God, when you went forth* in the column of fire during the night and in the column of cloud during the day *before your people, when you walked in the desert of Yeshimon*[b] *for ever.*

[a]There is no mention of unwedded parties in the Hebrew text.
[b]Yeshimon is a designation for desert places.

[9]When you gave the Law to your people, the *earth shook; even* the clouds of the heavens poured down dews of benevolence *before* the Presence of YHWH. This Sinai, its smoke arose like the smoke of a furnace, because being revealed upon it was the Presence *of YHWH, God of Israel.*

[10]When Israel heard your mighty voice, immediately their souls swooned. And immediately *you caused* to descend upon them dews of *vivification* and you projected *rains of benevolence, O God,* upon *your heritage.* And the assembly that *had grown slack, made firm.* [11]You made vivification re-appear in it; *you prepared* the armies of the classes of angels so as to do good *to the poor* of God. [12]The Word of YHWH *gave the words of the Law* to his people. But Moses and Aaron *announced* the Word of God to the *numerous* multitudes of Israel. . . .

[16]*The mountain* of Moriah has been chosen before me as a place where the patriarchs worshipped before YHWH, and it has been closed in the second place so that the house of the sanctuary be built thereon and the mountain of Sinai has been detached from there and chosen in the third place for the gift of the Law. *The mountain of Bashan* has been rejected. The mountain of Tabor, it is there that the miracle was wrought by Barak and Deborah. The mountain of Carmel, it is there that the miracle was wrought by the prophet Elijah. Now, they were running after each other and they were quarreling among themselves. The one said: "It is upon me that the Presence shall dwell." The other said: "It is upon me that the Presence shall dwell. And the Lord of the world, who hates the proud and whose dwelling is with the humble, grew angry against them and they were rejected and their summit was rendered like that of the mountain of Bashan. [17]God has said "*O mountains, why do you* leap from your sites? It is not my will to give the Law to proud, scornful mountains. Behold the mountain of Sinai is humble: the *Word of God wishes to place his Presence* on it. Only in the heavens, shall the Word of YHWH *dwell for ever.*"

[18]*Chariots of God,* there are two *myriads* of them in blazing fire; two *thousand* angels lead them. The Presence of YHWH *dwells* upon them, upon the mountain *of Sinai,* in *holiness.* [19]*You ascended* to the firmament, O Moses the prophet! *You have captured the captive,* you have taught the words of the

Law, you have given them as gift to the children *of men.*[c] But *the rebels* who become proselytes and convert to the Law, the glorious Presence of YHWH *dwells* with them.

[20]*Blessed be YHWH who each day* enjoins us by adding for us *commandments to commandments,*[d] the Mighty One *who is our liberator* and our aid forever. *God is for us* power and liberation. But before YHWH-God, death and the extinction of breath by suffocation are let loose upon the impious. [22]But *God shall shatter the heads of his enemies;* he shall let *fall out the hair* of a man who *walks* in his sins. . . .

[25]The house of Israel *has seen* the walk of your Presence on the sea, O God! They said: "The walk of our God, *king* of all time, is in *holiness:* [26]They arose at dawn and declaimed the hymn *after* Moses and Aaron, *who played music* before them, in the midst of holy *women playing the tambourine* with Miriam. [27]*Bless God* in the midst of the assembled peoples! Children in the womb of their mother sprung from *the race of* Israel exalt YHWH! . . .

[29]*Decree, O God, your might! Show yourself powerful, O God,* by dwelling in this holy House that you have made *for* us! [30]From your Temple, you shall receive the offerings; *in Jerusalem* resides your Presence! From their camps, *kings shall bring you presents.* [31]*Rebuke* the armies of sinners. You shall shatter them like the reed, this assembly of men who trust in calves, idols of the nations. His good pleasure is in the people that bestirs itself with exceeding willingness over the Law, which is more purified than money. *Scatter the war-desiring nation.* [32]The descendants of Ham, the blacks, shall come from Egypt to make themselves proselytes. The descendants of Cush shall hasten *to stretch forth their hands in prayer before God.*

[33]Kingdoms of the nations, give praise before YHWH! Give praise before YHWH from age to age in a world without end, he who is seated above the cherubs in the heaven of heavens since the beginnings. He himself, through his word, gives through his voice the voice of the spirit of prophecy to the prophets. [35]Render glory with the strength of God whose magnificence is upon Israel and whose might is in the heavens! [36]O God! You are formidable from the House of *your* sanctuary.

[c]Cf. Eph. 4, 8-13.

[d]It is the "yoke" of the Law, cf. Mt. 11, 28-30.

The Mighty one of Israel himself gives *strength* and *power* to his people. Let us declaim: "Blessed by God!

Most of the words of the Hebrew text find their equivalent in the Aramaic text, but the contexts are completely changed. The comparison of the people of God with the pagan peoples is subjacent to the whole. Above all, developments show an historical rereading of the psalm: the major events of Israel's history (Exodus, Sinai, conquest, remembrance of Elijah and even of Abraham's sacrifice) are inserted wherever a word permits such an insertion. But these insertions are constantly artificial. They depend upon a fundamental principle: the Word of God can speak of nothing else but the history of salvation. Consequently any useable text is adapted to refer to the concrete evolution of salvation history. Thus the haggada is constructed in a fashion that can enhance the literalness of the text without remaining enclosed within it.

# 48

# TARGUM OF PSALM 110

Instead of following the classic text of the rabbinic Bibles and of the London *Polyglot,* we shall take here the text of the manuscript prepared by Alfonso de Zamora for the Alcala *Polyglot,* a copy of which was followed by the Antwerp *Polyglot.* This psalm posed a problem to rabbinic theology because of its abundant utilization in Christian theology as a christological text (exclusively vv. 1 and 4). The messianic exegesis is resumed by the controversy that is related in Mk. 12, 35-37 and the parallel texts. But here it is systematically set aside for the benefit of the strictly historical exegesis that attributes the psalm to David.

> [1]*Through the instrument of David. Song. YHWH said* in his Word that he would give me mastery, in return of which *I seated myself* at the school of the Law *at his right:* "And wait *until*

*the time when I will place your enemies like a footstool at your feet."* (Another Targum). YHWH has said in his Word that He shall establish me prince of Israel. But YHWH has said to me "Wait *until* Saul, who is of the tribe of Benjamin[a] is removed from the world, *and I will place your enemies like a footstool at your feet."*

[2]*The sceptre of the power,* the Word of YHWH *shall transmit it from Zion and you shall rule in the midst of your enemies.*

[3]Your people is the house of Israel which devotes itself to the Law. On *the day* in which you shall wage war, you shall be sustained by them *in the splendors of holiness.* Mercies of God shall hasten toward you *like the descent* of dew. Your descendants shall sit in security.

[4]YHWH has sworn it through his Word and he will not disavow it. I am established master for ever for the world to come because of the justice through which I have been a just king.

[5]The presence of YHWH is at your right: *he has smitten kings on the day of his wrath.*

[6]He has been established as judge of nations; *he has smitten the heads of* kings *on the earth in a very great number.*

[7]From the mouth of the prophet, *on the way,* he shall receive an instruction. *This is why he shall raise his head again.*

The historical interpretation is facilitated by the rough literalness of many of the verses. This facilitates the neglect of the messianic interpretation in regard to vv. 1 and 4 which are the subject of dispute between Jews and Christians. What is particularly notable is the total disappearance of the royal priesthood in v. 4. Why? What is the targumist afraid of? Verse 3, which is very obscure textually, introduces a theme totally alien to the primitive text. In the second version of v. 1 the pun to which the word "right" gives rise with the allusion to Benjamin, "son of the right hand" is also noteworthy: it is clever, but the text is eluded. Verse 7, in its first stich no longer has anything to do with the primitive formulation.

[a]Benjamin = "son of the right hand."

# 49

# TARGUM OF THE SONG OF SONGS
## Song 7, 12–8, 3

The Targum of the Song of Songs, the reading of which was linked to the Passover festival, is practically a *midrash* of the book, an edifying explanation to which one can say that the "letter" read before serves as pretext. Behind the collection of love poems the targumists discover a series of allusions that allow a review of the "major" stages of Israel's history in so far as it is "salvation history." The personages of the dialogues are God himself, the prophets who speak in his name, the assembly of Israel, and the Messiah. The words of the book are redistributed among these new characters. Only a single example is retained here, one located toward the end of the book; the setting evidently envisages the end of sacred history with the coming of Messiah. The critical text is taken from G. Dalman's *Aramaische Dialektproben,* pp. 12f., by way of a comparison with the Manuscript of the Library of the University of Madrid.

(7) [12]Come, my Beloved! Let us go forth to the fields: we shall spend the night in the villages. [13]Early in the morning we shall come to the vineyards.

> We shall see whether the vine is sprouting,
> whether its branches are flowering,
> whether the pomegranates are in bloom.
> Then I shall make you the gift of my love.

[12]The children of Israel said to each other: "Let us rise early in the morning and *let us go* forth to the houses of the assembly and to the houses of the school, and let us seek in the books of the Law if the time of Deliverance for the people, the house of Israel, which is compared to the *Vine,* has arrived, so that they may be delivered from their exile. And we will ask the sages: Is the merit of the just, who are comparable to pomeranates, revealed before Yahweh, and has the appointed time arrived to ascend to Jerusalem, in order to give praise to the God of heaven and to offer holocausts and "holy victims"?

¹⁴"The mandrakes exhale their fragrance,
At our doors are all the best fruits,
the new as well as the old:
I have saved them for you, my Beloved.

¹⁴"When it shall be the good pleasure on the part of YHWH to deliver his people from exile, he shall say to the king Messiah: "Henceforth the appointed time of the exile is fulfilled. The merit of the just is *scented* before me like the fragrance of balm, and the sages of the generation are bent over the Law at the doors of the school; they pore over the words of the Law and over the words of the books. Now, arise! Now, receive the royalty that *I have saved for you.*

(8) Ah! If only you were a brother nursed at my mother's breast: meeting you outside, I could embrace you without people scorning me.

¹At that time, the king Messiah shall be revealed to the assembly of Israel. The children of Israel will say: "Come, be for us like *a brother,* and we will ascend to Jerusalem *and we will suck with you the* savor of the law of Moses as the babe *sucks the breasts* of its *mother.* For all the time when I had been wandering *outside* the country, when I recalled the name of the great God. I surrendered my soul to his divinity, and *the* nations of the world did not *scorn me.*

²I would lead you, I would usher you into the house of my mother.
You would teach me, I would make you drink a scented wine, my liquor of pomegranates.

²I will lead you, O King, I will usher you into the house of the Sanctuary, and *you shall teach me* to fear before YHWH and to walk in his way. And there, we will carouse at the festival of the Leviathan*ᵃ* and we will drink *an* old *wine* which has been preserved in its clusters since the day the world was created and *pomegranates* that have been prepared for the just in the garden of Eden.''

³His left arm is under my head and his right one embraces me.

³The assembly of Israel said: "It is I who am the elect among all nations, because I attach the *tephelin* to my left hand and

---

ᵃClassic theme: the monster Leviathan is to be killed and served to the elect. Cf. Is. 27, 1.

to my head because I fix the *mezuzah* to the right side of the door post[b] in front of the clapper, since no demon is permitted to harm me.

The poetic structure of the text, woven entirely of metaphors, kindles the ingenious imagination in regard to themes that the targumist has in mind, and which he had gathered from the global tradition of understanding this text. In this respect the Tg. of the Song represents the pinnacle of the creative *haggada*.

[b]These practices are modeled literally on Dt. 6, 8-9.

# 50

# STORY OF RUTH, THE PROSELYTE

The story of Ruth, a woman of Moabite origin who freely unites with the people of Israel and thus merits to become the ancestress of David and his lineage—up to the Messiah—is received favorably by the Targum. The language of the latter is mixed because the text is not very ancient. But is it not the quintessential example of a proselyte who forsakes her nationality in order to make herself a Jewess by adopting all the exigencies of the Law? The two passages used here will show the importance of this case from the point of view of mixed marriages in which a woman of pagan origins marries a Jew.

### Dialogue of Namoni and Ruth (1, 15-18)

[15](Naomi) said: "*Behold your sister-in-law has gone back to her people and to her divinity.[a] Return with your sister-in-law* to your people and to your divinity." [16]*Ruth said: "Press me not to leave you or to go away from you. For* I converted in order to become a proselyte." Naomi said: "We have the obligation to observe the sabbaths and the festival days, because we are forbidden to walk for more than two thousand cubits." Ruth

[a]Literally "her fear" (euphemism to designate the idol).

said *"Whither you go, I will go."* Naomi said: "We have the obligation not to lodge together with the Nations." Ruth said: "In whatever place you will lodge, I will lodge." Naomi said: "We have the obligation to observe the six hundred thirteen precepts." Ruth said: "Everything which your people observe, behold I observe it as though they had been my people previously." Naomi said: "We have the obligation not to practice alien worship." Ruth said: *"Your God shall be my God."* [17]Naomi said: "We have four death penalties for sinners: lapidation by stones, the act of burning by fire, execution by the sword and hanging on wood." Ruth said: *"In the manner that you will die, I will die."* Naomi said: "We have a burial place." Ruth said: *"It is there that I will be buried.* Therefore speak to me no further. *May YHWH do this unto me and add thereto, for it is death that shall bring about separation between me and you"* [18]When Naomi saw that Ruth was determined to go with her, she ceased to speak to her.

The text is amplified in a way which shows all the obligations that ensue for women come to Judaism through conversion. The enumeration of the 613 precepts is a classic rabbinic calculation. As regards the dialogue introduced into these verses, it is reproduced in the Babylon Talmud (tr. *Yebamoth.* 47b). It synthesizes the conditions under which women are admitted to Judaism. Ruth thus appears as the type of proselyte, subjected to the Law and therefore by the same token to the contingent sanctions provided by the Law. But Ruth is also going to marry Boaz, breaking with a prescription of Deuteronomy which forbids the admission of Moabites to the community of Israel. The targumist wonders how this could have come about.

### Dialogue Between Ruth and Boaz (2, 10-12)

[10]*Ruth fell face downward and prostrated herself* on *the ground. Then she said* (to Boaz): *"How have I found favor in your eyes, so that you take recognition of me?* And I, I am of an alien nation, among the daughters of Moab, a nation that is not pure for entry into the community of Israel. [11]*Boaz replied and said to her; "It has been shown to me* by the words of the sages that, when YHWH decided that, he did not decide for the people of the feminine sex, but only for men. Now, it has been told me in prophecy, that from you are to issue kings and prophets,

in consideration of *the goodness that you have shown toward your mother-in-law.* For you have supported her *after her husband died, and you have forsaken your divinity*[b] and your people, *your father and your mother, and the country of your birth, and you have* left in order to become a proselyte *and in order to dwell among a people that was unknown to you yesterday and previously.* [12]YHWH *shall reward you* with a good recompense in this world below on account of your good *work,* and *your retribution shall be complete* in the world to come from YHWH God of Israel, for you have come to make yourself a proselyte and *you put yourself under the protection* of the shade of the Presence of his Glory. And through this merit, you shall be saved from the judgment of Gehenna so as to have your share with Sarah, Rebeccah, Rachel, and Leah.''

The theme of Ruth's conversion is accentuated in this dialogue, so that the merit she deserves from this conversion associates her, a foreign woman, with the fate of the patriarchial women. A bit further on in the text it is said that among the blessings to be bestowed on her will be the birth of the king Messiah. This perspective can be compared with the place that Ruth occupies in the genealogy of Jesus, according to Mt. 1, 5.

[b]Literally: your fear.

# 51

# FROM THE DEATH OF JOSIAH
# TO THE COMING OF THE ROMANS
## Tg. of Lamentations 1, 18-19

The Targum of Lamentations tends to paraphrase the text stanza by stanza, then verse by verse, by placing them as much as possible within an adapted historical context. Here are two examples, drawn from the Lamentations 1. Verse 18 is divided into six lines, of which the second is applied to Josiah, and two others refer to the time from Josiah to the deportations of 597. V. 19 is applied to the destruction of Jerusalem and to the ensuing calamities.

> [18]YHWH said to the people, to the house of Israel, that people slaying by the sword shall pass upon its land. King Josiah went forth and drew his sword against Pharaoh the Cripple[a] in the valley of Megiddo, which had not been commanded and in regard to which he had not sought instruction from YHWH. This is why the archers shot arrows at King Josiah and he died there. When his breath had not yet left him, he murmured with his lips and said: "YHWH *is just, for I have transgressed his Word." Listen, now, all the peoples,* to the lamentation that Jeremiah pronounced in regard to Josiah: *"Behold my grief* that has come upon me after his death!" *My virgins and my young men are gone into exile.*
>
> [19]Jerusalem said, when she was delivered from the hands of Nebuchadnezzar: *"I have appealed to my friends* among the nations, those with whom I had concluded a covenant, so that they might aid me, *and they, they have betrayed me,* they have turned away in order to harm me. They are the Romans who have come with Titus and Vespasian, and they built camps against Jerusalem. *My priests and my elders have expired* in the midst *of the city,* for *they have sought* the sustenance *of bread* to eat for themselves, *in order to be able to sustain their lives."*

The story of Josiah is evoked in the same terms in the Targum of the Chronicles, 35, 20–25. The pharaoh is designated by use of the same play on words. The continuation of v. 18 is placed on the lips of Josiah before his death, and its end on the lips of Jerusalem after the deportation. Verse 19 is adapted from referring to the first siege to the refer to second, that of the Romans, without changing anything in the meaning of lines 2 and 3 of the stanza.

---

[a]Pun on the name of Pharaoh Neco (2 Kg. 23, 29).

# 52

# FROM THE MARTYRDOM OF ZECHARIAH TO THE MESSIANIC LIBERATION
## Tg. of Lamentations 2, 20-22

The disconnected character of the Lamentations permits the introduction, in the form of haggadic development, of the principal themes around which Jewish spirituality revolved in the rabbinic age. In the passage reproduced here, we shall find successively an allusion to the martyrdom of Zechariah, confused with the prophet of the same name (cf. 2 Chr. 24, 20-22; Mt. 23, 35) and an evocation of the ordeal of the Jewish people which is certainly an expression of the messianic hope.

²⁰*Look, YHWH, and behold* from the heavens! *Against whom have you turned thus? Was it necessary that the daughters of Israel eat* the fruit of their bowels, *the tender infants* who were *swaddled* in fine linen? Now, the Word replies to a decision of justice and speaks thus: "Was it necessary *to kill, in the house of the sanctuary of YHWH, the priest and the prophet,* as you have killed Zechariah son of Iddo, the high-priest and the faithful prophet, in the house of the sanctuary of YHWH, on the Day of Atonement, because he warned you not to commit evil before YHWH?

²¹*They lie on the ground* of places, *young people and old men* who were accustomed to sleeping on mattresses of wool and beds of ivory. *My virgins and my adolescents have fallen, slain by the sword: you have carried out* a slaughter *on the day of your wrath and you have not been sparing.*

²²May you proclaim freedom for your people, the house of Israel, through the hand of the Messiah, as you did through the hand of Moses and Aaron *on the day* of Passover, so that my young people may gather around from all the places to which they have been dispersed *on the* mighty *day of your wrath,* YHWH, *and there were among them neither saved nor escaped.*

> Those *I had* swaddled in fine linen and *that I had* nourished
> with royal viands, *my adversary has exterminated them.*

All the obstacles that the text presents are turned around in the
way that the primitive literalness is transformed by furnishing an
edifying meaning. It is not a question of a translation but of a
paraphrastic adaptation in which the traces of the primitive text
are easily discernible and traceable.

As regards Zechariah's martyrdom, the Targum of the Chronicles develops it in connection with 2 Chr. 24, 20, on which the
Tg. of Lamentations rests.

### Tg. of 2 Chr. 24, 20

[20]The spirit of prophecy before YHWH rested upon *Zechariah, son of the priest Yehoyoda,* when he saw the corruption
of the king and of the people who offered incense to the idol
of the sanctuary of YHWH on the altar of the Day of Atonement, and which prevented the priests of YHWH from perform-
ing the holocaust, the sacrifices, the daily oblation and the
supplementary offerings, according as is written in the Law of
Moses. *He stood up before the people and said to them: "Thus
has spoken YHWH: why do you transgress the commandments
of YHWH and come to naught? Because you have forsaken
the worship of YHWH, he shall forsake you."* [21]*And they re-
belled against him and stoned him, following the prescriptions
of the king, in the court of the sanctuary of YHWH.*

We see that the Tg. of the Chronicles is relatively literal, except when it develops the circumstances of Zechariah's martyrdom. But his father's name is given exactly, whereas the Tg.
of the Lamentations confuses it with the prophet of the same name
and who Mt. 23, 25 makes a son of Barachias, an unknown personage.

# 53

# FROM JOSIAH TO THE PUNISHMENT OF ROME AND THE COMING OF THE MESSIAH
## Tg. of Lamentations 4, 20-22

²⁰The king Josiah, who was dear to us like *the breath* of the spirit of life that is in *our nostrils* and that was instituted by the unction of the greatness of YHWH (variant: who was YHWH's *Anointed*), had been ensnared in *the net* of injustices of the Egyptians: *him of whom we said: "We shall live among the nations in the shade of* his justice."

²¹*Rejoice and exult,* Constantinople, city (variant: *daughter*) of Edom! which is built in the land of the Armenians (variant: *in the land of Uz*) by numerous multitudes who are of the people *of Edom. Upon you* also is to come retribution (= vengeance) and you shall be captured by the Hyrkanians and *upon you shall pass the cup* of malediction *and you shall be intoxicated and you shall be unprotected.*

²²After which, he shall *remunerate your iniquity, Assembly of Zion,* and you shall be liberated through the hand of the Messiah and of Elijah the high-priest, and YHWH *shall no longer deport you.* And at that time, *I will examine your faults;* Rome the impious that is built in Italy and that is full of multitudes from among the descendants of *Edom* (variant: *daughter of Edom,* city of Rome), and the Persians shall come and shall devastate you, because it has been *revealed* before YHWH in regard to *your sins.*

In v. 20, the allusion to the king is transferred from Joachin or Sedicias to Josiah, the only king whom one could praise. Later in the text Edom is identified with Rome, an identification classic in rabbinic literature. The allusion to Constantinople shows the late character of this text: it is a reaction to the laws of the Byzantine emperors, persecutors or pesterers of the Jews. Rome is not forgotten: there is an allusion to the century-old struggles between the Romans and the Parthians with the hope for a victory of the Parthians who will execute the Judgment of God. Compare the Tg. of Num. 24, 17-24, p. 60.

# 54

# SOLOMON'S DETHRONEMENT
## Tg. of Ecclesiastes 1, 12-14

The book of Ecclesiastes is attributed to Solomon. Why this pseudonym for a collection that the Targum presents nevertheless as a word of prophecy (Tg. 1, 1)? The author gives a curious elaboration of the text which makes it understandable why this king can proclaim the vanity of all things.

> [12]When Solomon was seated upon his royal throne, his heart was greatly uplifted on account of his riches. He transgressed the word of YHWH: he gathered numerous horses, chariots and riders. He accumulated lots of gold and silver and took a wife among the foreign nations. Immediately the wrath of YHWH waxed strong against him and he sent Asmodeus, the king of demons.[a] He chased him from his royal throne and he took away the seal from his hand, so that he became a wanderer and an exile in the world in order to rebuke him. And he moved about the cities of the provinces and the cities of the country of Israel, weeping and lamenting, and he said: *"I am Kohelet,"*[b] whose name was Solomon. Before that *I was* the *king* of Israel in *Jerusalem.* [13]*And I have yielded my heart in order to beseech* an instruction from YHWH at the time that he appeared to me at Gibeon in order to ask me what I desired from him. And I asked for naught save wisdom in order to discern between good and evil and sapience as regards *all that which has been wrought under the sun* in this world below.[c] And I

---

[a]Name of the demon in the book of Tobit.

[b]Literally: "Man of the assembly" (in Hebrew).

[c]Cf. 1 Kg. 3, 1-16.

saw all the works of the descendants of sinful humanity: *it is a bad task that God has given to the descendants of humanity as an affliction.* [14]*"I have seen all the works* of the descendants of humanity *which are wrought under the sun in this* world below, *and behold all is vanity and pursuit of wind."*

There is a certain paradox in describing the fallen king, while reaffirming that he had asked for wisdom and obtained the ability to discern what is good and what is evil. It is this fallen king who states that the works of men are but vanity. Thus the tone of Ecclesiastes throughout the book is explained by the perception of what is done in the world.

# 55

# THE REALISM OF EXPERIENCE
## Tg. of Ecclesiastes 8, 14-15

What is the result of this perception of the world? We retain a brief passage that attempts to define it:

[14]*There is a vanity of which* it is decreed that *it be wrought upon* the face of earth. The fact is that there are *just* to whom evil comes as though they were doing *sinful* works, and *sinners* to whom good comes as though they were doing *just* works. And I have seen in the Holy Spirit that the evil which overtakes the just in this world is not on account of their sins, but in order to discard from them the least sin so that their reward be perfect in the world to come, and that the good which overtakes the sinners in this world below is not on account of their merit, but in order to assure them a reward for the least act of justice that they have done, so that they eat their rewards in this world below and their share in the world to come be lost. *I have said* through my word *that that too is a vanity.* [15]*And I have celebrated the joy of the Law, since there is no good for man* in

this world under the sun, *if it is not to eat and to drink and to rejoice* in his work and in his share that is given to him by the Heavens, and that he not stretch forth his hand for pillages and violence; and that will lead him to peace in this world, and he shall receive a perfect reward *for the work* that he has accomplished in perfection, *all the days of his life which* YHWH *has given him* in this world below *under the sun.*

The observation of the world leads to a reflection upon the worth of individual acts. But it is to be noted that the targumist introduces into the text of Ecclesiastes a perspective of reward in the world to come which was totally alien to the book. The material joy of which the latter spoke is completed here below by the "joy of the Law." Thus the principles of rabbinic theology are projected upon a text whose canonicity was not achieved without difficulty. It is at this price that it assumes a value for edification in conformity with that of the Holy Scripture.

# 56

# EXCERPTS FROM THE TARGUM OF ESTHER

In the Targum of Esther the imagination gives itself free rein in order to pad the text of the novel. In the Tgs. I and II the amplifications are inserted into the literalness which Tg. III preserves. In Tg. II, on the contrary, everything is recomposed freely. It is not, strictly speaking, an explanatory *midrash.* It is a literary variation on the theme of the novel itself, with the insertion of totally new fragments. The Greek version had already begun this process. The Aramaic version pushed it to the extreme, by inserting alphabetical poems in several places. In the manuscript, Tgs. I and II are at times inverted. But Tg. II is recognizable by its language, which is in the Aramaic called "of Galilee" (that of the Palestinian Tg. of the Pentateuch). It is probably of late vintage. Moreover, the inserted alphabetical poems are very poorly

preserved and it is not always possible to restore the original text
on the basis of the variant manuscripts. Nevertheless these fragments have been chosen here as examples. The proposed text
results from the collation of five witnesses.

## Esther's Prayer

In chapter 5 the Greek version already interpolated a prayer
of Esther prior to her appearance before king Ahasuerus. The
Tgs. I and II do as much in a different form. Here we cite Tg.
I. This text connects with Est. 5, 1.

> And it came to pass on the third day, when Esther had prac-
> ticed three fasts day after day, that she arose from the dust and
> from the ashes, her figure remained bent and unstraightened.
> She made her preparations in the manner of queens. She donned
> a royal raiment adorned with fine gold of Ophir. It was a satin
> cloth of good quality silk spangled with stones and pearls that
> had been brought from the province of Phrygia. Upon her head
> she placed the beauteous crown of gold, and she slipped her
> feet into sandals of fine color. After which Esther began to pray
> and spoke thus:
> "You are the God of Abraham, Isaac, and Jacob, the God
> of Benjamin my father. It is not because I have done some-
> thing that is beautiful before you that I appear before this stupid
> king, but for your people, the House of Israel, so that they not
> be erased from the world, for it is for the sake of Israel that
> you have created the whole world (cf. Tg. of Is. 66, 2). For
> if Israel were to be erased from the world who would say: Holy,
> holy, holy three times a day? Just as you saved Hananiah, Mis-
> hael, and Azariah from the fiery furnace and Daniel from the
> lion's den, save me from the hand of this stupid king and grant
> me grace and favor in his eyes!"

### First Poem

Here begins a first poem of twenty-two stanzas beginning with
the twenty-two letters of the Hebrew alphabet.[a] The text is

---

[a]In the translation the 22 numbers correspond to these letters.

rhythmized, but its restoration on the basis of its different witnesses posed several problems. Nevertheless it is possible to end up with a likely result:

> [1]Esther with tears began to speak,
>   Asking a favor, she accordingly arranged her prayer:
> [2]I beg you, you who listen to prayers
>   listen to my prayer in this hour!
> [3]We are exiled and driven from our land,
>   and you have surrendered us because of our sins.
> [4]So as to carry out the Word that is written;
>   'You shall be sold to your enemies as slaves
> and servants.'
> [5]Behold we are sold
>   and there is no person to ransom us.[b]
> [6]And the law went forth to kill,
>   and we are all surrendered to the sword.
> [7]The descendants of Abraham are dressed in sackcloths,
>   and ashes are spread over their heads.
> [8]The fathers have sinned, in what have sinned their sons?
>   If we are annihilated, who shall praise you?
> [9]As for the families, if they have sinned before you,
>   what have the babes at the breast done?
> [10]The inhabitants of Jerusalem have shuddered in their graves,
>   because you have delivered their children to be slaughtered.
> [11]Like the clouds of heaven you make us disappear.
>   How fragile are the days of our joys!
> [12]To Haman the impious you have delivered us,
>   and to our adversaries so that we be slaughtered.
> [13]I recall before you the works of mercy;
>   I will begin with Abraham by saying:
> [14]You put him to the test by all kinds of trials,
>   you tested him and he was found faithful.
> [15]Help and sustain the descendants of your love,
>   so as to usher them into the seal of the covenant.
> [16]Demand account of our humiliation from Haman the impious,
>   and assure the punishment of the son of Hammedatha.
> [17]Draw vengeance from him through the hands of your people,
>   for he has wished to exterminate us all together.

[b]Repetition of Dt. 24, 68.

> [18]It is turmoil and distress for your people:
>    They are distressed in all their dwellings.
> [19]You have concluded with us an eternal covenant:
>    restore us, through the binding of Isaac![c]
> [20]Haman has paid a sum to the king so as to purchase us
>    for ten million silver talents.
> [21]Hear our voice and hearken to us,
>    and make us pass from anguish to tranquility!
> [22]Smite the powerful, smite Haman!
>    May there be no delay in his fall!

## Second Poem

A second alphabetical poem is connected to the first. In the course of transmission several secondary developments were grafted onto the stanzas. They are omitted here as much as possible.

> [1]Esther raised her voice and cried out in a loud shout,
>    and she complained in a bitter plaint.
> [2]With laments and tears she declaimed her words,
>    and in supplication she addressed her prayer.
> [3]Her throat was tight because of the cries from her mouth
>    and her eyes, closed because of her tears.
> [4]Esther reflected in her heart and said:
>    "Provided I do not appear before the king without
> being received by him!
> [5]Behold I am going to appear before the king
>    In order to ask a favor for my heritage.
> [6]And may an angel of grace precede me,
>    and may he usher in with me mercy and favor!
> [7]May the justice of Abraham enter before me,
>    and may the binding of Isaac sustain me!
> [8]May the amiableness of Jacob be placed in my mouth,
>    and the grace of Joseph be on my tongue![d]
> [9]His goodness is for the man who trusts in him,
>    and whoever leans upon him need not blush.
> [10]May he stretch forth to me his right and his left,
>    through which he has created the whole world!

[c] Cf. Tg. of Gen. 22.

[d] The remembrance of the patriarchs is constant in Jewish prayer.

[11]May all Israel ask favor for me
  for it is for them that I ask favor.
[12]To petition grace . . .[e]
  for your happiness, I have been appointed. (?)
[13]Whatever a man implores before the Holy One,
  his prayer is heard in times of his distress.
[14]Let us look upon the works of our fathers and do like them
  and He shall hearken to us.
[15]The left hand of Abraham was placed upon Isaac's neck
  and the right upon his knife.
[16]He willingly did the will of the Word,
  and he did not hesitate before your message.
[17]You opened the firmament window by window
  to give place to the angels above.
[18]They cried with bitterness and said:
  'Woe unto the world if he acts thus!'[f]
[19]I cry out before you, answer me,
  for you see the anguish of my soul.
[20]You have been called the Merciful One and the Compassionate One
  Listen to the voice of your Dove.
[21]Listen to our voice and answer us,
  and let us pass from anguish to tranquility.
[22]I have fasted three days before you:
  from here and henceforth what could I do?''

[2]Now it came to pass, when the king saw Esther standing in the entrance-hall, that she was granted grace and favor in his eyes. [3]And the guards of the king rose to kill Esther, [4]and the king held out to Esther his golden sceptre that he had in his hand, [5]and Esther drew nearer and rose to the height of the sceptre, [6]and the king said to her: "What is the matter, queen Esther, and what is your prayer?" For were it to be for half of my kingdom, I would grant it. [7]Esther replied and said: "My prayer and my request . . .''

The Hebrew text is thus rejoined. The additions that follow no longer concern Esther's prayer; there is no longer any need to reproduce them here.

---

[e]Mutilated stanza, impossible to reconstruct.
[f]Cf. Tg. Is. 33, 7-9, cf. p. 82.

## 57

# HAMAN'S GALLOWS AND THE DISPUTATION AMONG THE TREES
## Tg. of Esther 7, 10

The general arrangement of the narrative is respected after Haman has been denounced by Esther and the king decides to punish him. One of the king's guards counsels that he be hung on the gallows that had been prepared for Mordecai. It is then that Targum II amplifies the narrative considerably. In the first place Haman begs Mordecai to have pity on him, in a lengthy prayer in which there remain traces of an ancient alphabetical composition. Then in the face of Mordecai's refusal, Haman gives vent to his plaint and the trees begin a "disputation of prevailment" in order to determine which tree shall be chosen to serve as gallows. In the *Midrash Rabba* of Esther all are candidates and find good biblical grounds to buttress their demand. On the contrary, in the Targum, all challenge each other, except the cedar which has already provided a beam high enough to serve as gibbet for Mordecai. But the text presents itself in two different recensions. The one that is most common—that of the rabbinic Bible—gives an alphabetical poem in which only stanza 4 (*Dalethi*) is missing and in which the tree of the stanza following is not identifiable. Thus we see the following trees appear: the vine, the fig, the olive, the palm, the citron, the myrtle, the oak, the terebinth, the pomegranate, and the cedar, an enumeration slightly different from that of the *Midrash Rabba*. Two manuscripts however have destroyed this beautiful versified arrangement in order to reconstruct another Aramaic *midrash* on the same theme: the manuscript Or. 72 of the *Angelica* Library and the manuscript Hebr. 110 of the *Bibliothèque nationale* of Paris. It is the little known text that we have chosen to cite here, all the more so because it seems never to have been translated.

> When Haman saw that his words were not being listened to, he gave vent to plaints and tears of self-pity in the midst of the garden of the palace. He began to speak and said: "Hearken

to me, all ye trees and all ye shoots that I have planted since the days of yore, for the son of Hammedatha asks to be hoisted on the stake (?) of Bar-Pandera.[a] They all assembled and held a counsel: Haman would be hung on the top of the tree that would have a height of fifty cubits.

The VINE said: "I am too short and I am not fitted that he be hung from my topmost branch, for the assembly of Israel is compared to me. For it is thus written: 'You have uprooted a vine from Egypt,'[b] and, moreover it is from me that wine is taken for libations and blessings, and it is not possible that I be sullied by his corpse.'"

The FIG said: "I am not fitted that he be hung from my topmost branch, for the assembly of Israel is compared to me. For it is written thus: 'Like the early fruit on a fig tree in the good season . . .,'[c] and it is from me that the first fruits are taken and by me that Adam and Eve were clothed" (Ms. 110 only).

The POMEGRANATE said: "I am not fitted that he be hung from my topmost branch for the assembly of Israel is compared to me. For it is thus written: 'Your cheeks are like halves of pomegranates,'[d] and it is at the gathering of my fruits that the bell and the pomegranate on the lower hems of the coat of the high-priest are made,[e] and it is not possible that I be sullied by his corpse."

The OLIVE said: "I am not fitted that he be hung from my topmost branch for Israel is compared to me. For it is thus written: 'Verdant olive tree adorned with superb fruits: thus YHWH had called your name.'[f] And it is from me that oil is taken for the candelabrum in the House of the sanctuary;[g] the expert in mysteries has created me in order to remunerate the labors of the prophets and to invest the kings and the priests, and it is not possible that I be sullied by his corpse."

The CITRON said. "I am not fitted that he be hung from my topmost branch for it is to me that Abraham in his beauti-

---

[a] Denomination of Jesus in the rabbinic polemic from the 2nd century on.

[b] Ps. 80, 8 (in Hebrew).

[c] Hos. 9, 10 (in Hebrew).

[d] Sg. 4, 3, (in Hebrew).

[e] Cf. Ex. 27, 33.

[f] Jer. 11, 6 (in Hebrew).

[g] Cf. Lev. 24, 2.

ful old age is compared, and because it is from me that one takes in order to rejoice before the Lord of the world. For it is thus written: 'And you shall take for you, on the first day, fruits from the tree of honor . . .'[h] and it is not possible that I be sullied by his corpse."

The PALM said "I am not fitted that he be hung from my topmost branch for Isaac the just is compared to me. For it is thus written: 'The just shall sprout like the palm tree . . .'[i] and, moreover, because I am associated with the citron tree,[j] and it is not possible that I be sullied by his corpse."

The MYRTLE said: "I am not fitted that he be hung from my topmost branch for the just are compared to me. For it is thus written: 'And he stood up among the myrtles in the depth . . .'[k] And it is written: 'And he had brought *up Hadassah*,'[l] and it is from me that one takes for the joy and gladness of *Habdalah*[m] in the recitation of the Hallel and during the circumcision, and I am associated with the cedar tree and the palm tree in the joy of the festival,[n] and it is not possible that I be sullied by his corpse."

The WALNUT said: "I am not fitted that he be hung from my topmost branch for the exile community of Israel is compared to me. For it is thus written: 'I went down into the garden of walnut trees to see the young shoots of the ravine'[o] and the just of Israel are compared to me, and it is not possible that I be sullied by his corpse."

The APPLE said: "I am not fitted that he be hung from my topmost branch for the Lord of the world is complimented thanks to me. For it is thus written: 'As the apple tree among the trees of the forest, so is my Beloved among the young men,'[p] and the mountain of Sinai is called by my name, for

[h]Lev. 23, 40 (in Hebrew).

[i]Ps. 92, 13 (in Hebrew).

[j]Cf. Lev. 23, 40.

[k]Zech. 1, 8 (in Hebrew).

[l]Est. 2, 7, with a pun on Esther's name and that of the myrtle *(hadas)*.

[m]Prayer for the end of the sabbath.

[n]Cf. Lev. 23, 40. It concerns Lulab.

[o]Sg. 6, 11 (in Hebrew).

[p]Sg. 2, 3 (in Hebrew).

it is thus written: 'I awakened you under the Apple tree,'[q] and
it is not possible that I be sullied by his corpse.''

The OAK and the TEREBINTH said: ''We are not fitted that
he be hung from our topmost branches for it was underneath
us that Deborah, nurse of Rebekah,[r] was buried, and it is to
us that are compared the just. For it is thus written: 'A tenth
of them shall remain, and they shall again be delivered to thin-
ning like the oak tree and the terebinth whose residue of leaves
resembles dried out things, and up to that time they are moist
because their seed subsists: thus the exiled community of Israel
shall return to its land, for its plant is the holy seed,'[s] and it
is not possible that I be sullied by his corpse.''

The CEDAR said: ''I am the king of all the trees and taller
than all of them. I pray you, Guardian of Israel, expert in mysteries, that he be hung, Haman the impious, grand-son of Agag
the Amalekite, for it is from me that he had prepared the gallows, from the beam that Parshamdata his son had taken from
Noak's ark and had brought to his house. Haman had taken
it with joy and hidden it in his house in order to hang upon
it Mordecai the just and he had given the order to interrupt the
work on the great House of God that is in Jerusalem.[t] Thus
shall be fulfilled upon him what is written in the book of Ezra:
'And an order has been given by me that any man who would
transgress this word, a beam shall be torn from his house and,
set upright, he shall be put to death thereon, and his house
shall be transformed into a cesspool because of that transgres-
sion.' ''[u]

And immediately the Cedar cried out and raised its voice,
saying: ''Listen to me, all ye trees! I will deliver myself so that
Haman the impious and his ten sons be hung on the gallows
that he had prepared.'' And it said further: ''O God, you before all the kingdoms shall confess that you are God and that
there is no other God beside you! It is to you to whom it befits
to deliver your people from the hand of Haman who had risen
like a cedar, just as you delivered their fathers from the hand

[q]Sg. 8, 5 (in Hebrew).
[r]Cf. Gen. 35, 8.
[s]Tg. of Is. 6, 13, cf. p. 73.
[t]Cf. Ezra 4, 24 (in Aramaic).
[u]Ezra 6, 11 (in Aramaic).

of Sennacherib, the king of Assyria, who had raised his heart like a cedar,[v] and it is from me that the priests take the bough of cedar and throw it upon the pyre where the heifer is burning[w] in order to purify the stain. It is agreeable to me to carry out retribution for your people upon Haman the impious."

[10]*Thereupon they hung Haman and his ten sons on the gallows that he had prepared for Mordecai. And the anger of the* king that had waxed to the highest point was becalmed, and upon Mordecai was fulfilled what is written in the sacred books: "The just escape anguish and it is the impious who brings it upon himself."[x]

In relation to the alphabetical poem this construction is secondary, but it is also carefully organized. Each declaration is based upon the *midrash* of one or two biblical texts quoted in Hebrew, except at the end where the Targums of Isaiah and of Proverbs are quoted. Nowhere else do we obtain a better view of the interference between the Targum and the *midrash* than in the assemblage, which is very instructive for understanding the way in which the Bible is actualized in the rabbinic tradition. We cannot go into details here. But for each quotation, it would be necessary to refer to the *midrash* and to the Targum of the texts in order to make the necessary comparisons. The Bible is concerned with the past and the present at one and the same time: this is why it is interpretable through itself. The difference between the Jewish interpretation and the Christian interpretation derives from the fundamental principle that guides them. The former refers to the founding history of Israel in order to understand the meaning of which the texts can be pillars. The latter refers to the global event of Christ Jesus, historically come to pass and continued in the mysterious life of his Church. Here we have the quintessential type of Jewish "actualization," projected onto a text that lends itself to all haggadic developments.

[v]See Tg. Is. 37, 23.
[w]Cf. Num. 19, 6.
[x]Tg. Pr. 11, 8.

# CONCLUSION
# THE METHOD
# OF
# THE TARGUM

It is only at the end of a close reading that one can get an idea of the method of the Targum. As regards these texts, the oral preceded the written. This is certain as concerns the books of the Law (the Pentateuch), where the "canonization" of the Targum of Onkelos in the Jewish academies of Babylon made it supplant the Targum *Yerushalmi* (or Palestinian) of more ancient origin. But in all cases the Targum is not a simple literal translation. Even in cases when it comes close to literalness, it tends to introduce some explanatory glosses or some equivalences that "actualize" the biblical text. In order to judge this with a total exactitude, one should not trust the fragments that have been cited here. These have been systematically chosen as passages in which the midrashic elements considerably amplify the text. Nevertheless it has been verified at the beginning and at the end of the additions in question that the biblical text was always found intact, with slight modifications.

The same applies to a great part of the Pentateuch, above all to the Targum of Onkelos. As regards the prophets, all that remains are fragments from the *Yerushalmi;* perhaps these only existed for the passages utilized as liturgical readings alongside those of the Torah. To what extent there existed a sustained text of the prophets in Aramaic, before the sustained redaction of the Targum of Jonathan which abridged the preexisting fragments, as we have seen in some cases is impossible to know. The same can be said for the other "writings" that have been cited here (except for Job and Proverbs). In cases like those of the Song of Songs and of Esther, it is necessary to think of compositions written relatively late, in other words, of the Aramaic *midrash.* But it

141

is very difficult to establish a clear line of demarcation between the Targum and the *midrash,* this "search" for an explanation of the biblical text. It is clear that in many cases the *midrash* in its form of *halaka* (that obliges) or of *haggada* (that edifies with the aid of narratives) preceded the Targum at least in its traditional form. This general observation leaves the targumists free to elaborate the materials intended to edify the synagogal public: additions, explanations, puns, etymologies, remembrance of sacred history, projection of the content of prophetic oracles and their completion through later theological reflection, speculation on the two-fold destiny of the just and the sinners, etc. Thanks to this method, the listeners—later the readers—were placed before a "completed bible," rendered suitable for immediate edification.

In a certain number of cases, ancient parallels like those of the New Testament or of the *Book of Biblical Antiquities* (before 70) permit verification of the age of the collected materials. This applies in particular to the Targum *Yerushalmi,* for the work done on the Targum of Onkelos and the Targum of the Prophets has tended to align them with the rabbinic theology fixed at the level of the Mishna, of the Tosepheta and of the Tannait *midrashimiral* (end of the second century). This has been ascertained in several cases. But it must not be forgotten that the Targum, linked to the synagogal reading of the Torah, of corresponding prophetic passages, and of the "five scrolls" has remained eminently *traditional,* so that the reader of the New Testament can no longer ignore it any more than the one who is interested in ancient Jewish thought. The choice made here is not fully representative in the measure that it limited itself to greatly developed passages. May it at least give its readers the desire to know more of them in translation when it exists, as it does for the Pentateuch, thanks to R. Le Déaut. For that matter, why not in the original itself? Aramaic is no more difficult than Hebrew.

# BIBLIOGRAPHY

R. Le Déaut. *Introduction à la Bible, Nouveau Testament.* tome III, vol. 1: *"Au seuil de l'ère chrétienne."* Desclée, 1976, 109-10 and 224-25 (bibliography 235 and 245-46).

R. Le Déaut. *Introduction à la littérature targumique.* Rome, 1966 (in the process of correction).

R. Le Déaut. *Un phénomène spontané de l'hermeneutique juive ancienne: le"targumisme,"* Biblica, 52 (1971) 505-25.

R. Le Déaut. *La nuit pascale.* Rome, 1963, 1975.

R. Le Déaut and J. Robert. *Targoum du Pentateuque,* Translation of the two Palestinian recensions completed with introductions, parallels, notes and index, 5 tomes, coll. "Sources chrétiennes." Le Cerf, 1978-1981.

A. Diez Macho. *Le Targum palestinien,* in biblical exegesis and Judaism, published by J. E. Ménard, Strasbourg, 1973, 13-77 ( = *Revue des Sciences religieuses* 47 (1973) 169-231).

A certain number of the Targums cited here concern the Jewish hope of the Messiah. The texts in question are: 1, 9, 12, 22, 31, 33, 36, 43, 46, 48, 49, 50, 52, 53. Twelve other texts are cited by P. Grelot in *L'Espérance juive à l'heure de Jésus,* coll. Jésus and Jésus-Christ, nr. 6. Desclée, 1978, 198-234.

# TABLE OF BIBLICAL TEXTS CITED